AF226145

The Legend of Etana and the Eagle.

S. LANGDON, M. A.
Shillito Reader and Professor of Assyriology
in the University of Oxford.
Fellow of the British Academy.

The Legend of Etana and the Eagle

or the Epical Poem «The City they hated».

WIPF & STOCK · Eugene, Oregon

Wipf and Stock Publishers
199 W 8th Ave, Suite 3
Eugene, OR 97401

The Legend of Etana and the Eagle
Or the Epical Poem "The City they hated"
By Langdon, Stephen Herbert
Softcover ISBN-13: 978-1-6667-6694-3
Hardcover ISBN-13: 978-1-6667-6695-0
eBook ISBN-13: 978-1-6667-6696-7
Publication date 12/6/2022
Previously published by
Librairie Orientaliste Paul Geuthner, 1932

This edition is a scanned facsimile of
the original edition published in 1932.

INTRODUCTION.

The new material and successful joins of formely known tablets of the Etana Legend have made possible a more complete reconstruction of the text. Earlier editions are by P. JENSEN, *Keilinschriftliche Bibliothek,* VI, I pp. 100-115, and 581-588; P. DHORME, *Choix,* 162-181. The first attempt to edit the textes by E. J. HARPER, *Beiträge zur Assyriologie* II 390-418, exhausted the texts of the library of Ashurbanipal in the British Museum and remains an *editio princeps* for those texts. The two texts taken to America by the missionary Dr. W. F. WILLIAMS and unfortunately given into the hands of different owners (see pp. 5-6) belong to the same tablet and join. The Marsh tablet can no longer be traced at Amherst, Massachussetts, despite all efforts to obtain information about it by the late Professor G. F. MOORE of Harvard, who kindly interested himself for me in this matter; Dr. MARY INDA HUSSEY went to Amherst and endeavoured to trace the owner without success. I was unable to obtain a collation of either tablet, but the one at Pittsfield, Massachusetts is probably available and I should welcome the assistance of any Assyriologist who shall he able to collate it with the text which I have published here.

Translations based entirely upon the material and the arrangement of it by JENSEN and DHORME have been made by ARTHUR UNGNAD, *Die Religion der Babylonier und Assyrer,* and by ERICH EBELING, in HUGO GRESSMAN'S *Texte und Bilder,* 2nd edition, 235-240. The arrangement of the tablets was inevitably erroneous and consequently the argument of the poet much obscured. All the known material has been collected here; owing to the diverse publication of the texts in journals and books I found it difficult to use this myth for teaching purposes in class work and believe that a complete collection of the tablets in one place will be useful in this respect, as well as for the easy control of my edition by the reader. I have collated all the tablets published by HARPER, and had the help of Professor DOUGHERTY on the text of the Scheil tablet now at Yale. I am grateful to the editor of the *Yale Oriental Series* for permission to reproduce this tablet, now in the *J. Pierpont Morgan Library*, from the late PROFESSOR A. T. CLAY's copy, and to PROFESSOR SCHEIL for permission to include his new Susa tablet in order to make this edition as complete and useful as possible.

S. Langdon, Oxford, Nov. 14th, 1931.

The Legend of Etana and The Eagle.

or the Epical Poem « The city they hated ».

by S. Langdon.

The sources for the legend of Etana, deified king of the First Dynasty of Kish, who according to historical records was the thirteenth king after the Flood, are now extensive enough to enable Assyriologists to obtain a more clear understanding of the ideas and order of the argument in this myth. Hitherto the editions of the legend were based upon an erroneous arrangement of the sources, and the plan of the Babylonian poet has not been at all intelligible in them. Two serious lacunae still remain in the sources now available. Stating the situation in terms of the β edition [1]), five eights of Tablet I are missing. From the introduction of the legend it appears that the poem began by describing the conditions of society before kingship was founded, when the Igigi, gods of heaven and earth, hated mankind, but the Anunnaki, or gods of the lower world planned good things for them. But it was from the chief of the Igigi, father Anu, that kingship was sent from heaven, and upon kingship depended the civilisation of mankind. There is no explanation concerning the reason why Anu finally decided to bestow upon mankind the sceptre and crown of kingship, or how the Anunnaki overcame the original hostility of the Igigi to man.

The principal theme of this poem is that kingship is a divine institution and without it mankind had remained forever in barbarism. Kings rule by direct warrant from the gods of heaven and earth and they inherit this divine warrant from father to son. Great, therefore,

[1]) See p. 5. β edition is the single column Assyrian edition, and the α edition is the double column series, of which only one fragment has been recovered. The two early Babylonian fragments are, CLAY, *Morgan Collection* IV 2, a six? column edition, and the first tablet of that series; the SCHEIL, single column tablet, nearly complete, found at Susa.

was the disaster to that capital and kingdom whose ruler had no heir, and Etana of Kish had no heir. The poem seems to have begun, « The city they (the gods) hated », referring to Kish, capital of the first great kingdom of Sumer and Accad, whose king had no heir. That the city in question was Kish, is proved by the unplaced fragment, K 14788, which reads. *âlu-(ki) Kiš-(ki) i-bak-[ki]*, « The city Kish weeps ». *i-na lib-bi-šu...* « With in it (*there is lament*) ». *az-mu-ur...* « I have sung the ... ». And *iluE-ta-na* is mentionned twice in the following lines.

The longer part of the poem filling all of tablets II-IV is then taken up with the search for the plant of birth by Etana, who like Gilgamish in his search for the plant of life, fails in his quest. Etana loses his life in his daring adventure, but historical records bear testimony to his having a son who succeeded him on the throne at Kish. The quest for the plant of birth in high heaven, where Adapa was also received and offered the bread and water of life, was made possible by the assistance of the eagle, who carries him first to the plane of the planets, then to the plane of the constellations, and finally to the superior plane of high heaven. In the legend of Adapa, the only other mortal who is said to have ascended to the gate of Anu, there is no explanation as to how he made this ascension. It is clear that in Sumero-Babylonian mythology the plant of birth and the mystic bread and water of life, which bestow immortality, existed in high heaven with Anu, father of the gods. This conception of high heaven as the place where mortals might attain immortality is proved to be as early as the age of Hammurabi, by the old versions of the Adapa and Etana myths, and perhaps belongs to early Sumerian as seen on the seals. In so far as Babylonian mythology does provide this conception of heaven as a place to which certain privileged mortals might ascend and there find mystic plants and food of immortality, the Hebrew and early Christian legend of Enoch, who « walked with God and was not; for God took him », is dependent upon this Babylonian conception of a celestial paradise. Hebrew and Apocryphal tradition do not compel the inference that Enoch remained in the highest or third heaven, but that he was translated to high heaven in order to learn the sciences of astronomy, writing, mathematics and all the mysteries of the universe, after which he returned to earth, at least temporarily to teach men these secrets. [1]) Etana's ascension was by three stages to a third or highest heaven, but in late Palestinian tradition Enoch ascended on the wings of angels by seven stages, to the seventh heaven and the throne of God, corresponding to the heaven of Anu which Etana reached in his third flight [2]). The legend of three heavens is preserved in EBELING, KAR. 307, Obv. 30-33. « The *šamû elûti,* highest heaven, the stone *lu-lu-da-ta,* of Anum, the 300 Igigi therein he caused to sit. The *šamû ḳablûti,* middle heavens, the stone *saggilmut,* of the Igigi; the lord in the farfamed sanctuary, therein in the sanctuary of lapis lazuli sat; with byssus and sapphire within he made it brilliant. The *šamû šaplûti,* lowest heaven, the stone *ašpû,* of the *Lumaši* stars of gods he confined thereon ».

The seven *lumaši* stars, therefore, belong to the lowest heaven and must denote the seven planets here. The seven *lumaši* in CT 26, 45,7-10 = 41V 14-16 are Cygnus, Orion, Sirius, Centaurus, Aquila, Sagitarius, chosen according to BOLL, *Antique Beobachtungen,* 149 because they resemble the planet Venus in colour. See p. 42, n. *.

The Babylonian theory of an ascension to the third heaven, which is the highest, and where Anu father of the gods dwells, is clearly the one preserved in the *Testament of the Twelve Patriarchs,* a late Jewish apochryphal work at the end of the 2nd century B. C. This source is considerably earlier than the theory of seven heavens. The dream of Levi in the *Testament of the Twelve Patriarchs* preserves the Babylonian tradition [3]). The conception of a « plurality of heavens » is, therefore, not borrowed from Persian religion in late Hebrew and early Christian mythology but is Babylonian and traceable to at least 2000 B. C., in the sources of the Etana legend. The theory of immortal life in Paradise is also of Babylonian origin [4]), and

[1]) See CHARLES, *Apochrypha,* II 469, 68, 1-3. But St. Paul, Hebrews XI 5 distinctly states that Enoch was translated to heaven that he should not see death.

[2]) See FORBES and CHARLES in CHARLES, *Apochrypha* (*The Book of the Secrets of Enoch*) Vol. II, 432-442.

[3]) CHARLES, *Apocrypha,* II, 304.

[4]) LANGDON, *Babylonian Wisdom.* 29-30.

about all the ideas usually attributed by Biblical scholars to Persian sources are really Babylonian.

The legend of a man, carried to heaven on the wings of an eagle, survived in the legend of Alexander the Great, who in his search for the water of life in the Scythian land of darkness, is said, in the Ethiopic version based upon the Arabic version of Pseudo-Callisthenes, to have flown through the air by the help of three eagles.[1]) The oldest sources of the Alexander legend are in Greek. These relate how he mounted to heaven by yoking two great birds; having attached a basket to the yoke he climbed into it and ascended near to heaven, where a monster, a bird-man warned him not to seek to know the things of heaven. He was told to look downward at the earth; the earth appeared like a threshing floor and the sea like a serpent surrounding it. The texts and extensive literature of the Alexander myth will be found in *L'Ascension d'Alexandre,* par Gabriel Millet, *Syria* IV, 85-133 (unfinished). It is, however, no longer possible to regard Etana as the first king of the land[2]); for the wording of the early version (p. 11, 15) is precisely a translation of the Sumerian legend, which says that kingship descended from heaven with the first ante-diluvian king, and again with the first king of Kish after the Flood. Etana is the thirteenth king of the first dynasty of Kish, and there is no evidence that he appears, at all, in this poem until near the end of Tab. II (p. 33, 34). The opening lines of the poem do discuss the origin of kingship, but not in connection with Etana, unless the text, p. 7, l. 7, be restored to *E-ta-na.* This, after close examination of K. 2606, I regard as improbable.

The myth survived in omens, and in connection with Narâm-Sin. A. T. Clay, *Morgan Collection* IV, 13, 33 has, « If zone lines on the liver be like an eagle it predicts the augury given to ^{d}Etana, the king,

[1]) Sir E. A. Wallis Budge, *The History of Alexander the Great, being the Syriac Version of Pseudo-Callisthenes,* p. CVI. A similar tale of how an eagle rescued Gilgamish, when a babe he was cast from a tower, is told by Aelian. See OECT. II 12, n. 3. E. T. Harper, *Beiträge zur Assyriologie,* II 404-407, has collected other Armenian, Jewish and Mandaean tales of how the eagle aided women in child-birth.

[2]) Zimmern, KAT[3]. 556; Clay, *Deluge Story,* 34.

who ascended to heaven». Lines 34-5 contain two omens based on auguries given to Narâm-Sin.

List of Tablets[1]).

Old Versions.

1. *Morgan Collection,* published by A. T. Clay, *Babylonian Records in the Library of J. Pierpont Morgan,* Vol. IV, No. 2. Morgan Library, No. 1363. Also by Clay, *A Hebrew Deluge Story,* Pl. III. First published by V. Scheil, *Recueil de Travaux,* Vol. XXIII, 18ff. Partially edited by Jensen, KB. VI 581-588, and by Dhorme, *Choix de Textes Religieux,* 164-167; 174-175; Clay, *Deluge Story,* 37-8. It has apparently six columns, and is tablet I of that version, and ends shortly after the beginning of Tab. III of the β series. See p. 42. Obviously the old version of this six column type had two tablets; Tab. I corresponds roughly to I + II of the β Assyrian series, and to Tab. I of the α series. Reproduced from Clay's copy, with collation of Col. VI 9 by R. P. Dougherty, Pl. XII.

2. *Susa tablet.* Published by V. Scheil, *Revue d'Assyriologie,* XXIV 103-107. A small single colum tablet of the Hammurabi period. There are preserved 24 lines on the Obv. and 24 on the Rev. and from the restored Assyrian duplicates, pp. 20-21, little is broken away between Obv. and Rev. This is, therefore, a very small tablet, and indicates an early version made up of about eleven small tablets. Reproduced from Scheil's copy.

Assyrian Version, β edition.

1.*Pittsfield tablet.* Cited here as *Jastrow fragment.* Now joined to the Marsh tablet, thus forming a complete text of about two thirds of Tab. II. Published by Morris Jastrow, *JAOS.* XXX (1910) 101ff., with photograph. Republished by Carl Frank, *Studien zur*

[1]) In the Assyrian edition all single column texts are called β tablets, and double column texts α tablets.

Babylonischen Religion, frontispiece, and pp. 105-117. Now in the Berkshire Athenaeum, Pittsfield, Mass. U.S.A. Brought to America by the missionary, Dr. W. F. WILLIAMS, who was at Nineveh during the excavations of LAYARD. See Pls. I-III. β^1.

2. *Marsh tablet.* Published by MORRIS JASTROW, BA. III 363-384, with photograph. Now in possession of Dr. D. W. MARSH, Amherst, Mass., U.S.A. Brought to America by Dr. W. F. WILLIAMS. Now joined to the Pittsfield tablet. See Pls. I-III. β^1.

K. 1547. Fragment (β^3) near end of Tab. II Obv. and near top of Rev. Pls. V-VI. Published by E. T. HARPER, BA. II 443-5. Photographs, 503, 507. See also L. W. KING, *First Steps,* 206-214.

K. 2527. Fragment (β^2), end of Obv. and beginning of Rev. of Tab. II. Pls. IV-V. E. T. HARPER, BA II 439-441. Photographs, 503, 507. See also L. W. KING, *First Steps,* 206-214.

K. 2606. Fragment of double column (α) tablet. Numbered by scribe Tab. III, but certainly Tab. I of α series. The scribe's Tab. III is taken from some shorter tablet edition. Pl. VII. E. T. HARPER, BA. II 461-3. Photograph, Obv., 505.

K. 3651. Fragment (β^3) of Tab. IV along middle of left edge. Pl. IX. Obv.; here published for first time. Rev. (hitherto erroneously taken for Obv.) was published by E. T. HARPER, BA. II 459. Photograph, 503. Colour, reddish.

K. 8563. Fragment (β^1) from Obv. top, and Rev. end, of Tab. IV. Pl. IX. Published by E. T. HARPER. BA. II 449-451. Photograph of Obv., 509. Colour, dark grey. Not same tablet as 3651.

K. 8578. Fragment from top of Obv., Tab. III. Pl. VIII. See Bu. 79,7-8,43. Published by E. T. HARPER, BA. II 447.

Bu. 79,7-8,43. Fragment from top of Obv., Tab. III. Begins lower down than the duplicate, K. 8578. Pl. VIII. E. T. HARPER, BA. II 447.

Rm. 522. Fragment along left edge of Rev., Tab. IV. β^4, Pl. XI. E. T. HARPER, BA. II 459.

Rm. 2,454. Upper half of Tab. IV. β^2, Pls. X-XI. E. T. HARPER, BA. II 453-457. Photographs, Obv. 509, Rev. 505. Colour, reddish. Partially reproduced by L. W. KING, *First steps,* 200-3.

VAT. 10529, Assur fragment, published by ERICH EBELING,

Keilschrifttexte Religiösen Inhalts, No. 170. Reproduced by permission of the author. The Obv. belongs near the end of Tab. II, β series. See pp. 36-38. Pl. VI. The Rev., Pl. VIII contains a ritual, probably a preparation for the first flight and belongs to Tab III. See p. 53. Pl. VIII.

A.

Tablet I[*] of the two column edition + Tablets I-II of one column edition.

a) K. 2606, Obv. I 1-29; Morgan IV, No. 2, Obv. I 1-15.

Anunnaki fixed the fates of man, but Igigi are hostile setting a term on their lives. As yet no king and rulership. Sanctuaries had not been built, and Arallu was closed against men. Then rulership descended from heaven.

K. 2606. Pl. VII.

1. *âla i-ṣi-*[*ru?* ....]	1. The city they hated (?) ......
2. [......*id-*]*du-ú ilâni*	2. .... the gods placed ....
3. ....*ṣi-ru*(?) *ṣi-ru ul*	3. ...... *hostile, hostile* ....
4. *ina? pani-šù id-du-ú ilāni*	4. *Before him* the gods placed .. ..
5. ...... *lu? ú-kin-nu lib-ba ug?*	5. ...... they established a *disposition* of ...... [*in him*].
6. ...... *lu-u ri-é-um-ši-na*	6. .... their[1] shepherd ......
7. ...... *ta?-na*[2] *lu-u i-din-ši-na e*	7. ...... verily may he give them ....
8. *ši-bir-*[*ru*	8. a sceptre ......

[1]) Refers to *nišê,* people.

[2]) Photograph against *iluE-ta-na.* Restoration *E-ta-na* is hardly possible for kingship had not yet appeared.

*) But the colophon of K. 2606, the only text of the two column edition, is numbered tablet III, whereas it begins before Tab. II of the single column edition and ends with Tab. II of the single column edition. It must be, therefore, Tab. I of the α series.

9. *ra-bu-tum* ^{d}*A-nun-na-ki* [*ša-i-mu ši-im-tim*]	9. The great Anunnaki deciders of fate,
10. [*uš-bu*] *im-tal-li-ku mi-lik*[1]*-šu-nu* [*ana mātātim*]	10. sat pondering their plan [for the lands,]
11. *ba-nu-ú kib-ra-a-ti ša im-*[2]...	11. they who create the (four) regions, who ......
12. *ig-ri kâlu-šù-nu* ^{d}*Igigi nišê* [*isinna ana niši išimu*][3]	12. All of the Igigi hated[4] mankind; (and) they fixed a term upon mankind.[5]
13. *la iš-ku-nu* [*šar-ra-am kalu nišê apāti*]	13. [The pale faced people, all of them,] had not yet set up a king.
14. *i-na û-mi-šu-ma* [*la ka-aṣ-rat ku-ub-šum me-a-nu*]	14. At that time [no tiara had been worn, nor crown,]
15. *ù* ^{iṣu}*ḫaṭṭum uknâm* [*la ṣa-ap-rat*]	15. and no sceptre had been studded with lapis lazuli.
16. *la ba-na-a kib-ra-a-ti*[6] *ište-niš*......	16. The (four) regions had not been created together ......
17. ^{ilu}*si-bit-tum*[7] *eli um-ma-ni u-di-lu* [*bâbāni*]	17. The seven gods had locked the gates against the host (of mankind).

1) Copy *mi-lik-šù-nu*. Lines 9-10 = *Morgan* I 1-2.

2) *im* is certain. But *ša-kin* is expected from *Morgan* I 3. Has *IM* the value *kin?* See l. 3 p. 10. Read *ša-im* [*ši-im-tim*]?

3) Restored from ll. 4-5 below. For *isinnu*, festival, Syn. *simānu*, season, fixed period, term, see *PA-ŠE*(*i-ši-in*) = *išenu*, PBS. V 106 I 30; ZA. 8, 199,4 and *šel PA-ŠE-ba* = *eburi ina si-ma-ni-šu*, SBP. 52, 4 below, with Var. *eburu ina i-sin-ni-šu*, 206,5 = BL 26,17 and SBH. 21, 26-7, *i-si-in-šu*. See also Landsberger, *Kultkalender*, 22ff.

4) Nothing missing before *igri*.

5) Apparently they restricted mankind to short life and condemned them to labour. The phrase may be connected with Genesis 3,17-19 and Ps. 90,10.

6) Var. *parakku* l. 9 below. *išteniš* apparently « one beside the other ». See line 24. Cf. KB VI 52, 84 and note * below, p. 10.

7) The seven gods of hell, and attendants of Gira, the pestgod, Ebeling, *Era Mythus*, p. 2,29-4,36; whose fates were fixed by Anu. Here appa-

18. *eli da-ad-me u-di-lu*	18. Against the habitations they had barred the ....
19. *âl* ^{d}*Igigi šu-tas-ḫu-ru*	19. The city[1] of the Igigi they had surrounded ....
20. ^{ilat}*Iš-tar ri-é-a-*[*am*	20. Ishtar (then) a shepherd (*for the peoples sought*),
21. *ù šarram i-še-’-i*	21. and a king she searched for ....
22. ^{d}*In-nin-ni ri-é-*[*a-am* ....]	22. Innini a shepherd (for the peoples sought),
23. *ù šarram i-še-’-i*	23. and a king she searched for ....
24. ^{d}*En-lil i-ḫa-aṭ pa-rak-ki šame-e*	24. As Enlil looks over the cosmic chambers of heaven (and ....).
25. *iš-te-ni-’-e-ma*	25. he searched for ....
26. *ina ma-a-ti šarru* [*ul ib-ši*]	26. But [there was] no king in the land.
27. *šarru-ú-tu* [*ina šame-e ur-dam-ma*]	27. (Then) kingship (descended from heaven)[2]
28. *ub-lam-ma* [*libbi* ^{d}*En-lil šarram ana ša-ka-ni?*]	28. and [Enlil] bethought himself [to institute a king?][3]
29. *ilāni KUR*	29. The gods ....

rently each of the seven guards one of the seven gates on the descent to hell, and had not yet admitted the souls of men to enter the « land of no return ». See line 10 below, and p. 15,2.

[1]) The meaning is obscure. Note the title of the epic *âlu i-ṣi* (?) ......

[2]) According to the mythological dynastic list, OECT. II 8, this Sumerian text states that rulership descended from heaven in the beginning, in the time of Alulim = Alorus, first of the ten kings before the Flood, and again after the Flood, when Kish was founded and Ga-ur = Euēchoros became the first king of Kish. In this Kish dynasty E-ta-na, the shepherd, was the 13th king. The events mentioned under A a) clearly refer to the period before Alulim.

[3]) For restoration cf. *ublamma libba-ka ana šakan kamari*, EBELING, *Era Mythus*, p. 4,40.

Old Version, Morgan IV No. 2, Obv. I 1-15. *)

1. *ra-bu-tum* ^{d}*A-nun-na ša-i-mu ši-imtim*	1. The great ones, the Anunnaki deciders of fate,
2. *uš-bu im-li-ku mi-li-ik ša ma-a-ta-tim*	2. sat pondering a plan for the lands,
3. *ba-nu*[1] *ki-ib-ra-tim ša-ki-nu ši-ki-it-tim*	3. they who create the (four) regions, who found the « foundation », i. e. sanctuaries.
4. *ṣi-ru*[2] *a-na ni-ši i-lu I-gí-gu*	4. But the Igigi were hostile to the people,
5. *i-zi-nam a-na ni-ši i-ši-mu*	5. (and) they fixed a term upon mankind.
6. *šar-ra-am la iš-ku-nu ka-lu*	6. The pale faced people, all of

*) This must be tablet two of the old version since it begins with Obv. I 9 of Tab. I *a* of the Assyrian edition. See line 9 above. At present the contents of the entire first tablet are unknown and it is difficult to understand the plan of this epic which led up to the institution of kingship and the central episodes of the eagle and the serpent and the eagle and Etana. K. 3454, a long two col. tablet like K. 2606, gives a legend of Zû = the eagle of this epic, how he stole the tablets of fate from Enlil (and how they were recovered by Ninurta). Cf. KB. VI 48,39-40; 50,62-63; 52, 83-4, *libbanû parakkê, kibrat irbitti,* with lines 11 + 16 +24 above.

[1]) *banû* and *šākinu,* sing. participles, with plural subject, as also *na-ši* (var. *nāš*) *kakki, Epic Creat.* 89, 143, *et p.*; *šarrāni ālik maḫri*; see DELITZSCH, *Ass. Gram.*², § 174. The parallel passage, KB. VI 52, 84, *šitakkana maḫazi-ka,* proves that *maḫazu,* city, cult centre, is a synonym, or the plural *maḫazê* = the abstract *šikittu,* « institution », construction. For *šikittu,* sanctuary, cf. *ki-sĭg-ga* = *kisikkuki* (*elliti*), IV Raw. 19, no. 3 Obv. 9; SBP. 214, 24; ^{giš}*ki-sĭg-ga* = *šikittu ša bîti,* sanctuary of a temple, place of sacrifices to the dead, CT. 19, 43 A 9. ^{giš}*ki-sĭg-ga-bi-šú* = *ana šikitti-šu,* SBH. 119 A 3. The word in this special sense is clearly the Syr. *šĕkîntā,* Targumic *šĕkînā, šĕkîntā,* tabernacle, house, divine presence.

[2]) *ṣîru, ṣi-e-rum,* CT. 12, 48 B 19, adj. and noun, « hating », «hostile to», enemy. *ṣi-ru* adj. declined as a perm. verb. Cf. l. 12 above.

ni-ši e-bi-a-tim	them, had not yet set up a king.
7. *i-na ši-we-tim*[1] *la ka-aṣ-ra-at ku-ub-šum me-a-nu*	7. At that time no tiara had been worn, nor crown,
8. *ù ḫa-ad-du-um uk-ni-a-am la sa-ap-ra-at*	8. and no sceptre had been studded with lapis lazuli.
9. *la ba-nu-ú iš-ti-ni-iš pa-ra-ak-ku*[2]	9. The chambers[3] had not been created *together*.
10. *si-bi-ta ba-bu ud-du-lu e-lu ďa-ap-nim*[4]	10. The seven gates were locked against the *host* (of mankind).
11. *ḫa-ad-du-um me-a-nu-um ku-ub-šum ù ši-bi-ir-ru*	11. Sceptre, crown, tiara and staff
12. *ku-ud-mi-iš A-ni-im i-na ša-ma-i*[5] *ša-ak-nu*	12. were (still) placed before Anu in heaven,
13. *u-ul i-ba-aš-ši mi-it-lu-ku ni-ši-ša*	13. there being no royal direction of her[6] people.
14. *šar-ru-tum i-na ša-ma-i ur-da-am*	14. (Then) kingship descended from heaven
15.	15. ....

Long break

[1]) Arabic *suwai'atun,* moment; *suwā'un,* first part of the night = *šimê-tan,* evening.

[2]) In l. 16 above, *kibrati,* which is not a syn. of *parakku,* unless *parakku* is employed in a cosmic sense. *išteniš* here in the sense « at the same time ».

[3]) Here in sense of « throne rooms »?

[4]) But l. 18 above, *da-ad-me.* Read *da-ad-nim*(?) Or *dab/p-nu* = *ummānu,* l. 17 above? DHORME reads the ordinary word *dap-nu,* hero, valiant.

[5]) Here singular, gen. of *šamā'um* = Arab. *samā'un.* The gen. sing. *šamāi* > *šamê* is regular in early Babylonian, and the noun is treated as a plural (*šamê*) after the first dynasty, by analogy with the plural ending *ē* < *ī*. The sing. *šamā'u* > *šamû,* is then treated as a plural also. But the word in classical Accadian is singular.

[6]) Although Ishtar is not mentioned in this text, she does appear in the parallel Assyrian version, ll. 20-23 above.

b) Old version, Morgan IV, No. 2, Obv. II 1-13.

1. *li-ki*	1. Take thou ....
2. *mar-ḫi-is-[su*	2. His wife [1] ....
3. *la iḫ-?*	3. Not ....
4. *bu-šu*	4. Possessions ....
5. *ù a-na*	5. and to ....
6. *lu-ḫu (?)-*	6. ....
7. *il-li-[ik* ....]	7. He (?) goes ....
8. *PI- ?*	8. ....
9. *i-na*	9. In ....
10. *i-na*	10. In ....
11. *i-*	11. ....
12. *il-li(?)-[ik?*	12. He(?) goes ....
13. *ar*	13. ....

Long break of over 100 *lines*

The eagle and serpent become friends.

c) JASTROW fragment, Obv. 1-16. *) Susa version, SCHEIL, RA 24, 104, 1-3.

Pl. I 1-16.

1.	1. ....
2. [*al-*]*ka-ni-im ru-'u-a-tam i* [*ni-ip-pu-uš*]	2. *Come* [2], friendship [let us make].

[1]) [*mar*]-*ḫi-is-su* again on the fragment near the end of the epic, K. 8563 Rev. 2, and there obviously *marḫîtu* refers to the wife of Etana. If Etana's wife appears so early in the epic the legend must have passed over the entire ante-diluvian period, the Flood and the founding of Kish in a few lines and introduced Etana and his wife early in the argument, and before the story of the eagle and serpent begins. But when Etana first appears with certainty, p. 33, 34, he is described in a way to suggest that he had not been mentioned before. The references under A b) are, therefore, obscure.

[2]) Cf. p. 28, 17.

*) Here begins tablet II of the single column Assyrian (β) edition. and the second tablet of the single column Susa edition. About four lines

3. *ib-ri?* *it-ba-ru* *a-na-*[*ku* *u* *at-ta-*][1]	3. My *friend,* I and thou are companions.[2]
4. [*erû?*] *pâ-šu* *i-pu-šam-ma* [*i-zak-kar* *ana* *ṣîri?*]	4. The *eagle* opened his mouth, addressing the *serpent*: —
5. [*al-ka-m*]*a* *niš* *ša* *ru-'u-a-tu* *u* [*šul-ma-ni*[3] *i* *ni-it-ta-ma-a*].	5. « Come[4], let us swear to an oath of friendship and good will.
6. [? *la* *id-da-ru-*]*ma* *kab-tu* [*ni-iš* *iluŠamši*]	6. .... who fears not (the oath), heavy [is the curse of Shamash];[5]
7. *an-zil-*[*la*] *šá* *ilāni* [*ú-kab-ba-as*][6]	7. he treads upon the thing inhibited by the gods.
8. *al-ka* *ni-zak-pa-am-ma* [*ša-*] *da-a* *ni-il-li*]	8. Come we will arise and go up to the mountain.
9. *ni-it-ma-a* *irṣi-tim*[7]	9. We have sworn by the earth[8] ....
10. *ina* *ma-ḫar* *iluŠamši* *ḳu-ra-di* *ma-mit* *it-*[*mu-u*]	10. Before Shamash, the heroic, they took oath: —
11. *šá* *i-ta-a* *ša* *iluŠamši* [*it-ti-ḳu*][9]	11. « Whosoever transgresses the boundary of Shamash,
12.[9] *iluŠamaš* *lim-niš* *ina* *ḳa-at*	12.[9] May Shamash [smite him]

gone on Jastrow fragment. Tab. II of Assyrian β version begins earlier than Tab. II Susa. Over half of the Obv. and the whole Rev. of Tab. I are gone.

¹) Cf. Morgan IV, No. 2 VI 6 for restoration.

²) Here ends the address of the serpent? to the eagle? For reading *ib-ri,* see p. 23, 13.

³) For restoration see p. 23, 12.

⁴) Cf. p. 28, 17.

⁵) Uncertain; restored from p. 23, 13.

⁶) Cf. OECT. VI 41, 35 + 47; Ebeling, KAR. 45, 11. Cf. p. 32, 31.

⁷) For this construction, with direct object of thing sworn by, cf. *šarru ila uštimmê-šu,* The king caused him to swear by god, King, *Boundary Stones,* p. 73, 14.

⁸) I. e., we swore, « may the earth ...... us if we break the oath ». Cf. *it-ma-ma ša nāri ul išatti mê-šu,* « He swore, 'the waters of the river he will not drink' », KB. VI 62, 32. See l. 17 under d).

⁹) Restored from Marsh *frag.* Obv. 13 = p. 20, 40.

ma-ḫi-ṣi [lim-ḫu-uṣ-su]	calamitously by the hand of a smiter.
13. *šá i-ta-a šá ilušamši [it-ti-ḳu]*	13. Whosoever transgresses the boundary of Shamash,
14. *li-is-su-šu-ma ni-ri-[ib-ta-šu-nu ša-du-u]*	14. May the mountains remove afar their[1] entrance from him.
15. *iṣukakku mur-tap-pi-du*[2] *eli-šu [li-ši-ir]*[3]	15. May the swift weapon[4] fall upon him.
16. *giš-par-ru ma-mit iluŠamši lib-bal-ki-tu-šu-ma [li-ba-ru-šu]*[5]	16. May the trap and curse of Shamash pass over him and entrap him ».

Susa version[6], Obv. I 1-3.

(Whosoever transgresses the boundary of Shamash),

1. *li-iḫ-li-iḳ-šu ṭu-ú-du a-ja*[7] *u-ta*[8] *ḫarranam*	1. May the route be lost for him and may he find not the road.

[1]) The verb *is-su* is plural, hence *šadû* is treated as a plural here. Variant Susa, Obv. 2 has a better text. See below.

[2]) Else-where *murtappidu* is used with *eṭimmu*, ghost, King, *Magic*, 53, Obv. 15; Clay, *Morgan* IV 18, 7; *Šurpu* 4, 21; KAR. 21 Obv. 10; *akkannu murtappidu*, the swift wild ass, KAR. 96, 22.

[3]) For *ašaru*, fall upon, Prt. *išir*, v. *Epic Creat.*, 118, n. 4.

[4]) The ordinary association of *murtappidu*, in n. 2 above, suggests rather « snare » which lies in wait for an animal.

[5]) Restored from Marsh frag. Obv. 12. See p. 20, l. 39.

[6]) This tablet probably began with line 13 above.

[7]) For *aja* (> *ai*) negative, see Ungnad, VAB. VI 249; Zimmern, KL. 214 V 12; *a-a-ja i-du-ru*, let them not return, *Keilschrifttexte aus Boghazköi* I 3, Rev. 31.

[8]) Probably I[1] prt. of ותה = אתה. The root is *watû*; see *izkim* = *wa-tu-ú*, Delitzsch, *Glossar*, 27. The prt. is apparently *uta*, JRAS. 1921, 176, 9. In Assyrian *ita; ta-a-ta-a*, *Harp. Lett.* 46, Rev. 19. Imp. *a-ta*, ZA 7, 27, 3.

2. *li-ik-la-šu ne-ri-ib-ta-šu šă-du-ú*	2. May the mountain close its entrance against him [1].
3. *ka-ak-ku-um mu-ur-ta-ap-pi-du e-li-šu li-še-ir*	3. May the swift weapon fall upon him.

d) **They go to the mountain each hunting for the others food.**

Jastrow frag. Obv. 17-27.

17. *iš-tu ma-mit it-mu-u irṣi-tim*	17. After they had sworn an oath by the earth ....
18. *iz-zaḳ-pu-nim-ma ša-da-a e-lu-ú*	18. They arose and went up to the mountain,
19. *ûmakal i-na-ṣa-ru iṣur[ati]* [2]	19. each day keeping watch [3] for *birds,*
20. *rêmu* [4] *pu-ri-mu erû i-bar-ram-ma*	20. the eagle catching wild bulls and asses,
21. *ṣirû ik-kal i-ni-'ú* [5] *ik-ka-lu mārē-šu*	21. the serpent eating, and when he withdrew his children ate;
22. *ar-mi* [6] *ṣabâti ṣîru i-bar-ram-ma*	22. the serpent catching mountain goats and kids,
23. *erû ik-kal i-ni-'u ik-ka-lu mārē-[šù]*	23. the eagle eating, and when he withdrew his children ate;

[1]) The mountain, i. e., the land of the dead. See also p. 8, 17.

[2]) Read *ḪU-MEŠ?* For restoration see B a) l. 3; p. 42.

[3]) For this use of *naṣāru,* cf. I^2, *ni-ta-ṣar,* « we are on the lookout for (an astronomical phenomenon) », THOMPSON, *Reports,* 21,6; 76 Rev. 1.

[4]) *gud-am.* Here *gud* is determ. as im KAH. 84, 124. See Susa tab. Obv. 8.

[5]) *nī'u,* « to turn back », transitive, with *irtu,* «to turn back ones breast», to turn around, retreat. Hence *nī'u,* with *irtu* omitted, intransitive, as in *la ni-i,* who retreats not, KING, *Magic,* 21, 40. The verb here is subj. sing.

[6]) FRANK'S suggestion that *armu* = Syr. *arnā* ist undoubtedly right. See also BROCKELMANN, *Vergl. Sem. Grammatik* I 231 *β.*

24. *sa-ap-par-ri*[1] *di-da-ni erû i-bar-ram-ma*	24. the eagle catching antelopes and *stags*,
25. *ṣîru ik-kal i-ni-'-ú ik-ka-lu mārē-[šù]*	25. the serpent eating, and when he withdrew his children ate;
26. *[nim-ru mi-in-]din(?) ḳak-ḳa-ri ṣîru i-bar-ram-ma*	26. the serpent catching panthers and *marsh*-lions,[2]
27. *[erû ik-kal i-ni-']-ú ik-ka-lu mārē-[šù]*	27. the eagle eating, and when he withdrew his children ate.

Susa tablet, Obv. 4-11. **Each produce offspring. They go to the mountain, the serpent hunting for the eagle to eat.**

4. *ma-mi-ta-am ut-ta-ma-am-mu-u*[3]	4. (After) they had sworn an oath,
5. *na-ap-ḫa-ar i-ru-ú na-ap-[ḫa]-ar ul-du*	5. All (their children) were conceived, all (their children) were born.
6. *i-na ṣilli(lí) zi-ir-bi-tim*[4] *ú-li-id ṣîru*	6. The serpent begat in the shade of the *elm*.

[1]) Loan-word from *šeka-bar, šenbar*, CT. 14,1,6; CT. 11, 39, K. 4151 II 20.

[2]) Variant, Susa tab. Obv. 10, *ni-im-ra-am mi-in-di-am*. As SCHEIL observed *mindiam* must be an error for *mindinam*· The form *mi-in-te-mu* occurs, KBö. I 52,7 = Sum. *ug*, with *nib* = *nimru*. The usual Sum. is *ur-gūg* = *girru*, lion, *min-di-nu*, CT. 14, 1 A 4+6, and *ur-gūg-kud-da* = *dumāmu*. *dumāmu* is probably derived from *damāmu*, to wail and *midinu* from *madānu*, to wail. See also *ur-gūg* with *Ug-banda* = *nimru*, CT. 27,22,13. Since *gūg* = *elpitu, šišnu* etc. rush, sedge, the natural inference is that *ur-gug* means «dog of the rushes», lion which infests the marshes, but the chase here is on the mountains! Cf. *ur-mağ ḳaḳ-ḳa-ri*, « lion of the soil », CT. 14 A 9; *Gilgamesh Epic* XI 313, and JENSEN's note KB VI 518; MEISSNER, MVAG. 1904, 201. In any case the Syriac « lion of the earth », « lion of the dust », is an erroneous rendering of the Greek χαμαίμηλον (for χαμαιλέων !), « earth apple »; I. Löw, *Aramäische Pflanzennamen*, No. 33.

[3]) II^{3} of *tamû*, for *uttanammû* (Scheil). This line corresponds to l. 17 above.

[4]) SCHEIL regards *zirbitu* as a dialectic form of *ṣarbatu*, elm.

7. *e-ru-ú it-ta-la-ad i-na ṣi-ri-šu*	7. The eagle begat on his peak.
8. *ri-ma ša-ap-pa-ra ṣîru i-ba-ra-am-ma*	8. The serpent caught a wild bull and an antelope,
9. *e-ru-ú i-ku-ul i-ku-lu ma-ru-šu*	9. and the eagle ate, his children ate.
10. *ni-im-ra-am mi-in-di-am ṣîru i-ba-ra-am-ma* [1]	10. The serpent caught a panther and a *marsh*-lion.
11. *e-ru-ú i-ku-ul i-ku-lu ma-ru-šu*	11. and the eagle ate, his children ate.

e) **The children of the eagle grow up. The eagle plots to devour the young of the serpent and fly to heaven and descend to earth.**

Jastrow fragment, Obv. 28-32 + Marsh fragment, Obv. 1-9. As joined up on Pl. I, ll. 28-36. Susa tablet, Obv. 12-21.

Plate I.

28. *erû im-ḫu-ur* [2] *ú-kul-ta: mārē erî ir-bu-ú i-ši-ḫu*	28. The eagle received food: the children of the eagle grew up, they became large.
29. *iš-tu mārē erî ir-bu-ú i-ši-ḫu*	29. After the children of the eagle had grown up and become large,
30. *erû lib-ba-šu li-mut-tu ik-pu-du-ma*	30. and the eagle's heart had plotted evil,
31. *ik-pu-ud-ma lib-ba-šu li-mut-tu* [3]	31. his heart plotted evil.

[1]) See l. 26 above.

[2]) In the copy, BA. II 379,1, *ID-ḪU* must be conjectured. From the Photo of the Jastrow frag., where it joins the Marsh frag., I see *ur,* und Frank sees *lu.* My restoration is based on the old version, ***Morgan,*** IV, Rev. VI, 3, ***e-ru-ú ma-ḫi-ir ú-ku-ul-ta-am.***

[3]) There is a tautology in lines 30-31, compared with the Susa tablet, line 14 below, which is inexplicable. The join of the two tablets on Pl. I is certain. The scribe seems to have combined two variant editions.

32. *a-na ad-mi ša ru-'u-a-šù a-ka-li uz-nu-šù iš-kun*	32. He set his mind upon devouring the young of his friend.
33. *erû pâ-šu i-pu-uš-ma i-zak-kar ana [mārē-šù]*[1]	33. The eagle opened his mouth, saying to [his children]: —
34. *mārē ṣîri-mi*[2] *lu-ku-lu ana-ku: ṣîru-mi lib(?)-ba? ......*[3]	34: « Lo, I will devour the children of the serpent; the serpent ....
35. *e-li-ma i-na ša-ma-mi uš-[ša-ab-ma]*	35. I will ascend and in heaven dwell.
36. *ur-rad i-na ap-pi iṣ-ṣi-ma a-kal in-ba*	36. I will descend and eat fruit on the top of a tree. »

Susa tablet.

12. *iš-tu ma-ru-šu ir-bu-ú [i-ši-ḫu]*	12. After his children had grown up [and become large].
13. *ga-ap-pi ?* [.....] *ir-?* .... [*ab-ri?* ....]	13. and they had ...... wings and had .... [pinions?],[4]
14. *e-ru-ú i-na li-ib-bi-šu [li-mut-tam ik-pu-ud]*	14. the eagle plotted evil in his heart, saying: —
15. *ma-ru-ú-a-mi [ir-bu-u i-ši-ḫu]*	15. « My children have grown up and become large,

[1]) Restored from K. 1547 Obv. 10. See section k).

[2]) *mi*, particle attached to introductory word of direct discourse, or at end of the first phrase. See Thureau-Dangin, RA, 11, 154; « *ul aššat-mi atti* » *iḳabbi*, Clay, *Morgan*, IV 52,8; cf. RA. 23, 143, No. 5, 6; *Code Ham.* § 11, *la-ni-ik-ki-me*; AJSL. 28, 220, 40, *nâki-mi-i*. *Et passim*. Cf. p. 46, 27.

[3]) L. 34[b] is not in the parallel passage of the Susa tablet. It must have given the reason why the eagle supposed that devouring the young serpents would result in some benefit to himself. It is possible that some astronomical reference occurred here. See note on line 17 below.

[4]) *gappi* is acc. pl. in this text. The nom. pl. would be *gappū* here. Scheil reads *iš-še-ir-ru*, « the wings were developed », but I do not know how this meaning was obtained.

16. *it-ta-al-ku i-še-ú-[ni ....]*	16. they shall go and seek .... *for me* [1].
17. *i-še-ú-ni šă-am-ma-am [ša a-la-di-im?]* [2]	17. they shall seek the plant [*of* birth] *for me* [1].
18. *ù* [3] *ma-ru* [4] *ṣîri lu-ku-[ul anaku]*	18. And I will devour the children of the serpent.
19. *e-te-el-li-ma i-na [ša-ma-mi]*	19. I will ascend and in heaven
20. *uš-ša-am-ma [ur-rad ina appi iṣṣi-ma a-kal in-ba]*	20. dwell, [I will descend and eat fruit on the top of a tree];
21. *ma-an-nu-um šă [itti-ja išannan?]* [5]	21. Who is there [that shall rival me?]»

f) **A wise young one of the eagle warns him not to devour the young serpents.** Cf. section l), p. 28.

Marsh fragment 10-13 = Pl. I 37-40. Susa tablet, Obv. 22-24.

Pl. I 37-40.

37. *ad-mu ṣi-iḫ-ru a-tar ḫa-si-sa : a-na erî abi-šù amata [izakka-]ár* [6]	37. A young child, one exceedingly wise, spoke a word to the eagle, his father: —
38. *la ta-kal a-bi še-e-tu šá iluŠamši i-ba-[ar-ka]*	38. « Eat not, my father, the net of Shamash will entrap thee.
39. *giš-pár-ru ma-mit iluŠamši*	39. The trap and curse of Sha-

[1]) But *ni* in this period should not be used as dative of the 1st per. sing. See Ungnad, ZA. 17, 360 n. 1. Scheil adheres to the strict application of the classical syntax and takes *u-ni* as emphatic plural.

[2]) In section B e) Etana asks the eagle to give him the plant of birth, implying that the eagle had found it.

[3]) So Scheil.

[4]) Sic!

[5]) Cf. p. 49, 8.

[6]) The colon in this line does not mark the end of a sectence but the end of a line on the early copy; see below ll. 22-3. For *KA-MU-ár* see *a-ma-tum i-zak-kar,* K. 1547 Obv. 22, section l), p. 28, 18.

ib-bal-ki-tu-ka-ma i-bar-ru-ka	mash will pass over thee and entrap thee.[1]
40. *šá i-ta-a šá* ^{ilu}*Šamši it-ti-ku* ^{ilu}*Šamšu lim-niš ina ka-at* [*ma-hi-și imahhaș-su*][2]	40. Whosoever transgresses the boundary of Shamash, by the hand [of a smiter] will Shamash [smite him] calamitously. »

Susa tablet.

22. *ad-mu-um* [*și-ih-ru-um a-tar ha-si-sa*]	22. A young child, one exceedingly wise,
23. *a-na e-*[*ri-i a-bi-šu amatam izakkar la-ta-kal*]	23. spoke a word to the eagle, his father: — « Eat not,
24. *a-bi* [*še-e-tu ša* ^{ilu}*Šamši i-bar-ar-ka*]	24. my father, the net of Shamash will entrap thee ».
....	....

g) **The eagle heeds not the words of his son, but devours the young of the serpent**, End of section lost between β^1, Obv. end and β^2, Obv. top.

Marsh fragment, Obv. 14-20 = Pl. II 41-47. Susa tablet Rev. 1-8.*

Pl. II 41-47.

41. *ul iš-me-šu-nu-ti-ma ul iš-ma-a* [*zi-kir māri-šu*][3]	41. But he listened not to them, he listened not to the address of his son.

[1]) See p. 14, l. 16.

[2]) See p. 13, l. 12.

*) Obviously this tablet is a small one and only the end of section f) is lost at the end of Obv., and the beginning of section g) at the top of Reverse.

[3]) Restored from Marsh frag. Rev. 9 = Pl. II Rev. To what does *šunuti* refer? Apparently the eagle's children had all appealed to their father through the one who is called *atarhasis*. Or can this pl. object refer to *gišparru, šêtu, mamit*? In this case *šemû* would have the meaning « heed », « pay attention to », and would disagree with its meaning in *ul išmâ*.

42. *ú-ri-dam-ma e-ta-kal mārē [ša ṣîri]*	42. He descended and devoured the young ones of the serpent.
43. ...... *šù(?)-a-ti ina ḳir-bit û-me: ṣîru [it-ta-di ma-ḫa-ar* ....]	43. ...... this one during the days; the serpent he cast down before ....
44. *[i]-na-ši bi-lat-su*[1]) : *ina*	44. taking away his offspring:
45. .... *ma ḳin-na-[šu iš-muṭ]*	45. he .... and [tore] his nest [assunder.][2])
46. *[ṣu-up-] ra-nu-[uš-šu ḳa-pár-ra* ....]	46. With his talons ....
47. .... *nu*	47. ....

Susa tablet, Rev. 1-8.

....	....
1. *?-ru-tu(?)*[3])	1. ....
2. *li-la-tu*	2. Night ....
3. *ṣira i-ku-šă-[am-ma*[4])	3. The serpent he brought ......
4. *ši-i-ra ta(?)*	4. *Morning* ....
5. *ṣîram it-ta-di ma-ḫa-ar*	5. The serpent he cast before ...
6. *ip-pa-li-is la-aš-šu-ú [ma-ru-ú-šu]*[5])	6. He looked and his children were not.
7. *zu-up-ra-nu-uš-šu ḳa-par-ra-am?*	7. In his talons ....
8. .... *šă-ma-a-a*	8. .... heaven ....

h) **The serpent weeps before Shamash.** K. 2527 Obv. 2-13. Susa tablet Rev. 9-24.

[1]) *biltu*; see p. 36, 40. Line 43 is restored from Susa tab. Rev. 5.

[2]) Cf. K. 2527 Obv. 6. under h).

[3]) Scheil reads *za-ru-tu.*

[4]) For *kâšu,* to bring, v. JRAS. *Centenary Volume,* 1924, 40, l. 4.

[5]) Cf. l. 17 below.

K. 2527, Obv. 2-13. *)

2. *ṣîru i-na* ....[1]) [*i-bak-ki*]	2. The serpent wept in (*sorrow*) :-
3. *at-kal-kúm-ma* [^{ilu}*Šamaš ḳu-ra-du*]	3. « I put my trust in thee, [o heroic Shamash!]
4. *a-na erî šu-*[*ul-ma-ni a-na-ku aš-ru-uk*]	4. To the eagle [I gave a gift of goodwill.]
5. *e-nin-na ḳin-ni*	5. But now my nest he has ......
6. *ḳin-ni-ja šam-tu i-*[*na ṣu-up-ri-šu?*]	6. My nest is torn assunder [*by his talons*].
7. *sa-ap-ḫu ad-mu-ú-a la*[*ššû mā-rū-a*][2])	7. My little ones are scattered, [my children are not].
8. *ú-ri-dam-ma e-ta-kal* [*li-da-ni-ja*]	8. He descended and devoured [my offspring].
9. *lum-nu šá i-pu-šá-an-ni* ^{ilu}*Ša-maš* [*lu ti-di*]	9. The wickedness, which he has done, O Shamash, [thou knowest].
10. *a-maš-ša*[3]) ^{ilu}*Šamaš še-it-ka ir-ṣi-tum* [*ra-pa-aš-tum*]	10. Surely, O Shamash, thy net is the wide earth.

*) Since this fragment is near the end of a single column (β) edition, I thought at first that it may have joined the Marsh fragment at the bottom of the Obverse, but this suggestion is proved to be erroneous by the relation of the Reverse. Note that K. 2527 Rev. 15ff. carries signs which stand also on Marsh frag. Rev. 2ff. See Pl. II, Rev. 2ff.

[1]) Susa tablet, l. 9 below has an adverb, ... *ru-uš*. Hardly *ma-aḫ-ru-uš*, « in his presence », refering to *šamâ* in l. 8; if so then l. 8 belongs to section h) and *ina mah-ri-šu* is the restoration here. Cf. *ḳabluš, Epic Creat.* p. 136, 65; *i-du-uš,* 94, 15.

[2]) Written *nu-*[*tuk-ú*]*?* See lines 17-9 of Susa tablet, below.

[3]) See V Raw. 16 Rev. A 28, *a-maš-ša* in list of adverbs, *kima, appuna, tašâma, mindi.* For restoration see l. 21 of Susa tablet below.

11. *giš-pár-ru-ka* [1]) *šamu-ú* [*ru-ḳu-ti*]	11. Thy trap is the [far-away] heaven [2]).
12. *i-na še-ti-ka ai u-ṣi* [*erû*]	12. From thy net may the eagle not escape,
13. *e-piš lumut-tim iluZu-ú* [3]) *mu-kil* [*limut-tim a-na ib-ri-šu*]	13. the evil doer, Zû, he that upholds evil against his companion. »[4])

Susa tablet, Rev. 9-24.

9. [*ṣîru* ......]*ru-uš* [5]) *i-ba-ak-ki*	9. The serpent wept in ....
10. ....*il-la-ka ki* .... *šu*	10. ....
11. *at-ka-la-ak-ku-um-ma iluŠa-maš ḳú-ra-du*	11. «I have put my trust in thee, O heroic Shamash,
12. *a-na e-ri-i šul* [6])*-ma-ni a-na-ku áš-ru-uk*	12. To the eagle I gave a gift of goodwill.
13. *a-du-ur-ma* [*ni*]*-iš-ka ú-ka-ab-bi-it* [7])	13. I feared and honoured the oath by thee.
14. *li-mu-ut-ta ú-ul ú-ki-il a-na ib-ri-ja*	14. I upheld not evil against my companion.
15. *šu-ú ḳí-in-na-šu šă-li-im-ma za-pi-iḫ ḳí-in-*[*ni*]	15. As for him, his nest is left in peace, and my nest is scattered.
16. *ḳí-in-ni ṣîrim da-ma-mi-iš*	16. The nest of the serpent has

[1]) Susa tab. l. 21, below, *gi-iš-pi-ir-ra-ka*. This is surely dialectic. Cf. *giš-pa-ri*, CLAY, *Morgan* IV 8, 26. *giš-par-ri*, KAH. II 84, 67. *giš-pa-ru*, IV Raw. 16 A 11 + 26.

[2]) Restoration by SCHEIL.

[3]) Susa tab. *anzilli!* The Assyrian edition identifies the eagle with *Zû*, which does not seem to be in the original text.

[4]) Restored from l. 24 below, Susa tablet.

[5]) Read *ma-aḫ-ru-uš?* See p. 22 n. 1.

[6]) SCHEIL's conjecture is probably right.

[7]) See p. 13, line 6 and p. 34, l. 36.

i-wi[1])	become as a *damamu*[2]).
17. *šă-al-mu ad-mu-šu la-áš-šu-ú ma-ru-ú-a*	17. Safe are his little ones, but my children are not.
18. *ùr-da-am-ma i-ta-ka-al li-da-ni-ja*	18. He descended and devoured my offspring.
19. *lum-na il-li-ka*[3]) *iluŠamaš lu ti-di*	19. Evil he commits, thou knowest, O Shamash.
20. *še-it-ka ḳí-ir-bi-tu ra-pa-[aš-tu]*	20. Thy net is the wide field,
21. *gi-iš-pi-ir-ra-ka [šamû ru-ḳu-]tu*	21. Thy trap is the [far-away heaven].
22. *i-na še-ti-ka ai [u-ṣi] e-ru-ú*	22. From thy net may the eagle not escape,
23. *e-pi-iš li-mu-[t-ti ù an]-zi-il-li*	23. the doer of evil and shamefulness,
24. *mu-ki-il li-[mu-ut-]ti a-na ib-ri-šu*	24. he that upholds evil against his friend. »

i) **Shamash tells the serpent to conceal himself in the carcass of an ox, on which the eagle will descend, and be seized by the serpent.** K. 2527 Obv. 14-20 + Rev. 1-8; K. 1547, Obv. 1-9.

K. 2527, Obv. 14-20.

14. *un-ni-ni šá ṣîri [ina še-mi-*	14. When he heard the supplica-

[1]) For this root הוה = *emû*, cf. *aweliš i-wi,* « he has come into the state of being a man », i. e., *iš* (with *emû*) for *ana* pregnans. SCHOTT, MVAG. 1925, 2, p. 11, denies this pregnant sense of *iš* with *emû* and claims that it has only the weaker meaning *kima,* « has become *like* ».

[2]) This word is a hapax. Probably from *damāmu,* to wail.

[3]) But *lumnu ša ipuša-anni,* p. 22, l. 9 above. For this sense of *alāku,* cf. *alkakatu,* doing, pl. *alkakati; il-ka-ka-tu-šu,* KAH. II 13 I 8. *alkatum ešîta,* « the rebellious affair », OECT. VI 89, 49; *al-ka-tu-uš,* « his achievement », 98, 100. *alaku* is used here in the sense of *begehen* in German. For *alaktu,* « what one does », state of affairs, doings, cf. R. C. THOMPSON, *Reports,* 120, 3; 121, 4. See DELITZSCH, HW. 67 *a* 4).

šu][1])	tion of the serpent,
15. *ilu Šamšu pâ-šu i-pu-šá-am-ma a-na* [*ṣîri i-zak-kar-šu*][2])	15. Shamash opened his mouth, [saying to the serpent] :-
16. *a-lik ur-ḫa e-ti-*[*iḳ ša-da-a*][3])	16. « Pursue the route, pass over the [mountain].
17. *uk-ta-as-si-ka ri-*[*ma*]	17. I will bind thee a wild bull.
18. *pi-te-e-ma lib-ba-šu* [*ka-ras-su šu-ṭu-uṭ*][4])	18. Open his interior, rend his belly.
19. *šu-ub-ta id-di* [*i-na kar-ši-šu*]	19. Take up thy abode in his belly.
20. [*mim-mu-ú*] *iṣ-ṣu-rat ša-ma-me* [*ú-ra-da-ma ik-ka-la ši-i-ra*]	20. Every kind of bird of the heavens will descend and devour the flesh[5]).

K. 2527, Rev. 1-8. K. 1547, Obv. 1-9.

1. *erû it-ti-ši-na* [*ik-kal ši-i-ra*]	1. The eagle will devour the flesh with them.
2. [*ša*][6]) *la i-du-ú-ma* [*lu-mu-un-šu*][7])	2. *Since* he knows not *his danger,*
3. *nu-ru-ub šêri iš-te-*[*ni-'-i: sa-da-a-ti*[8]) *it-ta-na-al-lak*]	3. he will seek for the entrance to the flesh, he will walk about on the *entrails.*

[1]) Restoration by E. J. HARPER, BA II 392, 14.

[2]) Cf. K. 1547, Rev. 17; p. 32, 29.

[3]) Cf. 1547, Obv. 11 = line 9 p. 27; also 37, 42.

[4]) Cf. K. 1547, Obv. 13. *šaṭaṭu,* p. 27, 11. Ethiopic *šaṭaṭa,* to disrupt.

[5]) Restored from p. 27, 13.

[6]) Or restore *as-šum? la* is clear on the tablet.

[7]) Here begins K. 1547 Obv., fragment from lower part of a single Col. tablet. Cf. l. 14 under j). Traces on K. 1547, 1 are not favourable to this restoration.

[8]) *sadātu,* or *sâdatu?* ALBRIGHT, RA. 16, 187 n. 3, wishes to connect this word with סוידא in the Aramaic story of Ahikar, COWLEY, *Aramaic Papyri,* p. 215, 88, where it is said that the lion ***devours* the hart in the** secrecy of the *sawîdā.* DR. COWLEY, *ibid.,* 235 suggest « lair », « den » or something similar. As in Aramaic, so here, the word is a hapax and the

4. *a-na ku-tu-um lib-bi uš-ta-ma-am-me* [1])	4. He will flutter over the loins.
5. *a-na lib-bi ina e-ri-bi-šu at-ta ṣa-bat-su i-na kap-pi-šù*	5. When he enters into the interior seize him by his wings.
6. *nu-uk-kis kap-pi-šu ab-ri-šù ù [nu-pal-li-]šù* [2])	6. Tear off his wings, his pinions and his talons.
7. *bu-ḳu-un-šu-ma i-di-šù* [3]) *ana šu-ut-ta-ti* .... *uš*	7. Strip him and cast him into a pit ... .
8. *mu-ut bu-bu-ti ù ṣu-um-mi* [4]) *li-mu-ta*	8. May he die the death of hunger and thirst. »

two words can hardly be identical; for the context here clearly requires an anatomical word· See p. 29, 13.

[1]) *me* is clear on K. 1547,4; the Marsh tablet, BA. III 381, 13, probably has *a-na kutum libbi; ku-ut-mu li-ib-bi*, Syn. *libbu, gabidu* = *kabittu*, KBö. I 51, Obv. 8 *uzumà-úr-ra* = *ku-tum lib-bi, digšu: uzumà-šag-ga* = *digšu*, following *ḫinṣu*, loins, ZA. 30, 290, 14-15. Var. *mà-ur-ra* = *ku-tum libbi*: *ḫinṣu*, ZA. 33, 18, 14 = 26 II 19, *á--úr-ra* = *ku-ut-[mu] libbi* and *digšu*. *uštamammê*, probably III/II² of *mamû* = מיח ? for *mawāḥu*, Arabic ميح, form V *jactavit corpus et in latera movit in incessu*. See p. 29, 13.

[It is clear that this word does not rest on good textual authority. Only *uš-ta-ma-?-me?* on K. 1547 seems clear on that text (collation). Photograph of Marsh tab. Rev. 13 is not decisive.]

[2]) Restored from Marsh frag. Rev. 22. *nuballu šuparruru* means in any case « to spread out a net, set a trap », KB. VI 122, 10; 123, 37. Tiglathpileser, *ša nu-ba-lu-šu kima urinnu eli māti-šu šuparruru*, King, AKA. 94, 57-8. Here *nubalu* is spread out like an *urinnu*. But *gišaz-bal* = *nâbaru, nabartum ša nêši*, cage for trapping animals, Meissner, SAI. 2559 with *gišaz-bal* = *erinnu*, 5558, hence *erinnu* (cage) = *urinnu; nâbaru* from *abāru*, to entrap; *gišgiš-gar* = *šigarum*, cage, *gišaz-bal* = *na-bal-[lu?], erinnu*, CT. 12, 44 Rev. 2-3. Hence *nabal[lu]* or *nabal[tu]* = *nabartu*. Cf. *r* > *l* in *ulamkib* = *urakkib*, PBS. I¹, 113, 56; *iltešû* = *irtešû*, Ebeling, KAJI. 8, 13. Is *nuballu*, cage, net, for *nubarru?* Clearly then if *nupallu*, here, is the word *nupal-lu* = GAB(du), CT. 12, 11 B 16, the root is *napālu* = GAB(du), said of scratching the eyes, *ibid.*, 7. *napālu* to scratch, erase, *nupallu*, claw, instrument for digging out the eyes. *nuballu*, trap, cage, seems to be an entirely different word. What is *nub/pallum ummāni imaḳḳut*, the ....of (my) army shall fail? Boissier, DA. 9, 30 = Boissier, Choix, 188.

[3]) Var. K. 1547, Obv. 8, *id-di*. [4]) K. 1547, 9, *ṣu-mi*.

j) **The serpent obeys Shamash and conceals himself in the carcass of the ox.** K. 2527, Rev. 9-15; K. 1547, Obv. 10-18. Marsh fragment Rev. -2 (Pl. II).

K. 2527 + 1547.

9. *a-na zi-kir* ^{ilu}*Šamši ḳu-ra-di* [1]) : *ṣîru il-lik- i-ti-iḳ ša-da-a*	9. At the word of the heroic Shamash the serpent went and passed over the mountain.
10. *ik-šu-ud-ma ṣîru a-na ṣi-ir ri-mi*	10. The serpent came upon the wild ox.
11. *ip-te-e-ma lib-ba-šù ka-ra-as-su iš-ṭu-uṭ* [2])	11. He opened his interior, he rent his belly.
12. *šu-ub-ta id-di* [3]) *i-na kar-ši-šù*	12. He took up his abode in his belly.
13. *mim-mu-ú iṣ-ṣu-rat šá-ma-me* [4]) *ú-ri-da-ma ik-ka-la ši-i-ra*	13. Every kind of bird of heaven descended, devouring the flesh.
14. *erû lu-mu-un-šù i-[da-]*[5]) *a-ma*	14. Will the eagle know his danger?
15. *it-ti mārē iṣ-ṣu-ri ul ik-kal ši-i-ra*	15. Will he not devour the flesh with the birds?

k) **Eagle sees the ox and tells his young ones that he will descend and eat.** K. 2527, Rev. 16-17; K. 1547 Obv. 19-20. Marsh frag., Rev. 3-4 (Pl. II).

[1]) K. 1547, Obv. 10, *du*.

[2]) See line 18 above, p. 25.

[3]) K. 1547, 14. *it-ta-di*.

[4]) Ibid., 15, *mi*.

[5]) For restoration, cf. l. 2 above. *lu-mu-un*, first traces on Marsh frag. Rev. 1.

16. *erû pa-a-šu i-pu-šá-am-ma* [1]) *i-zak-ka-ra ana mārē-šù*	16. The eagle opened his mouth saying to his children [2]) :-
17. [*al-*]*ka-nim-ma* [3]) *i ni-rid- ma šîr rîmi an-ni-e i ni-ku-la ni-nu*	17. « Come, let us descend and let us devour the flesh of this wild ox ».

l) **A wise young one of the eagle warns him not to feed upon the ox.** K. 2527, Rev. 18-19; K. 1547, Obv. 21-23; Marsh frag., Rev., 5-6. Cf. section f).

18. *ad-mu ṣi-iḫ-ru a-tar ḫa-si-sa* [*a-na erî abi-šu*] *a-ma-tum i-zak-kar* [4])	18. A young child, one exceedingly wise, spoke a word to the eagle, his father :-
19. [*la*]*tūr-rad a-bi min-di ina lib-bi rîmi an-ni-e ṣîru ra-bi-iṣ*	19. « Descend not, my father, perchance the serpent lies in the interior of this wild ox ».

m) **The eagle heeds not the words of his son, but feeds upon the ox. He is seized by the serpent.** Cf. section g).

K. 2527, Rev. 20-21; K. 1547, Obv. 24; Marsh frag., Rev. 7-15. Lines now numbered from Marsh fragment, Pl. II 7ff.

7. *erû it-ti-šù* [........][5]) *ama-tum i-ḳab-bi*	7. The eagle spoke with him self .... (saying ?) :
8. ....(?) *a* .... *ki-i-mi ik-ka-* ....[6])	8. « .... how ....? »

[1]) K,1547, 19, *i-pu-šam-ma.*

[2]) Cf. p. 18, 33.

[3]) Cf. p. 12, 2; 13, 8.

[4]) Cf. p. 19, 37; p. 39, 1.

[5]) Uncertain. Dhorme restores *it-ti lib-bi-šu* after Streck, *Assurbanipal,* II 44, 25, *iḳbi itti libbi-šu*. Lines 7-8 do not appear in the parallel passage at the beginning of section g). The restoraton is impossible from the photograph, where *six* signs occur between *ti* and *KA* = *amatum*. See Pl. II 7. K. 1547 Obv. 24, [*a-ma-*]*tum.*

[6]) A collation would probably yield the text of this line.

9. *ul iš-me-šu-nu-ti-ma ul iš-ma-a zi-kir-māri-šù*	9. But he listened not to them, he listened not to the address of his son.
10. *ú-ri-dam-ma it-ta-ziz ina eli ri-me*	10. He descended and stood upon the wild ox.
11. *erû ip-kid šíra iš-te-ni-'-i šà pa-ni ù ár-ki-šù*	11. The eagle inspected the flesh, he searched in front and behind.
12. *iš-ni-'i ip-ḳid šíra iš-te-ni-'i -i šà pa-ni ù ár-ki-šù*	12. Again he inspected the flesh, searching in front and behind.
13. *sa-da-a-ti it-ta-na-al-lak a-na ku-tum lib-bi uš-ta-ma-am-a!*[1])	13. He walked about on the *entrails*. He fluttered over the loins.
14. *a-na lib-bi ina e-ri-bi-šù:*[2]) *ṣîru iṣ-ṣa-bat-su ina kap-pi-šù*	14. When he entered into the interior the serpent seized him by the wing (saying):
15. *ṭú-ub tuš-ṭe-en-ni ṭú-ub tuš-ṭe-en-ni*	15. « Is it good that thou tastest me? Good that thou tastest me? »[3])

n) **The eagle pleads for mercy**. Marsh fragment, Rev. 16-17. Pl. II. *).

16. *erû pâ-[šù] i-pu*[4])*-šá-am-ma ma a-na ṣîri i-zak-kar-šù*	16. The eagle opened his mouth saying to the serpent:
17. *rîm-an-ni-ma kima e-ri-ši nu-*	17. « Have mercy upon me and I

[1]) See note on p. 26, l. 4. *Re mamû* = Arabic *mâḥa,* PROFESSOR D. S. MARGOLIOUTH assures me that the fundamental meaning of Arabic m-j-ḥ (= m-w-ḥ in Accadian) is to « grope after », « move gently ».

[2]) See p. 19, n. 6.

[3]) For *tuš-ṭe-em-ni? ṭêmu,* used as a verb?

[4]) So photograph, clearly, as for example K. 2527, Rev. 16.

*) CLAY, *Morgan* IV 2, Rev. V (?) 1-2 contains beginnings of two lines from this part of the poem.

dun-na-a lut-lim-ka [1])	will bestow upon thee a dowry like a bride groom ».

o) **The serpent refuses to release him and recounts his evil conduct. He despoils him and casts him into a pit.**

Marsh fragment, Rev. 18-24. *Morgan* IV 2, Rev. V (?) 3-9.

Pl. II, Rev. 18-24.

18. *ṣîru pâ-šu i-pu-šà-am-ma a-na erî i-zak-kar-šù*	18. The serpent opened his mouth, saying unto the eagle :-
19. *ú-maš-šar-ka-ma* *ilu**Šamaš e-li-nu ki-i ap-pal*(?)	19. « If I release thee how shall I *answer* Shamash on high?
20. *še-rit-ka i-saḫ-ḫu-ra a-na muḫ-ḫi-ja*	20. Thy punishment would turn upon my head.
21. *šà a-šak-ka-nu-ka a-na-ku še-ir-ṭa*	21. Is it I who puts punishment upon thee? »
22. *ú-nak-ki-is kap-pi-šù ab-ri-šu nu-pal-li-šù* [2])	22. He tore off his wings, his pinions and his talons.
23 [*ib-ḳu*]*-un-šu-ma id-*[*di-šu ana šu-ut-ta-ti*][3])	23. He stripped him and threw him into a pit.
24. [*mu-ut*] *bu-bu-ti ù ṣu-*]*mi-i*[4]) *i-ma-*[*at-mi?*]	24. « He will die a death of hunger and thirst », *he said.*

Old version, Morgan IV 2, Rev. V (?), 3-9.

3-4. *ṣi-ru pa*[*a-šu ipušamma ana erî i zakkar-šu*]	3-4. The serpent opened his mouth, speaking to the eagle,

[1]) *Morgan* Rev. V (?), 1, *lu-ša-*[*at-lim*]; l. 2, *ṭa-ab* ......

[2]) See p. 26, 6.

[3]) Traces of *a-na-šu-ut-ta-ti* on Jastrow frag. Rev. 1. See Photo. JAOS 30, p. 131. See p. 26, 7.

[4]) Sic! *ṣumû* on this text. See Pl. III 24. See p. 26, 8.

5. *ma-a* [1]) *ú-ṣab-[bit-ka šum-ma u-maš-šir-ka]*	5. saying, « I have seized thee; [if I release thee,]
6. *ši-ri-it-[ka i-saḫ-ḫu-ra a-na muḫ-ḫi-ja]*	6. thy punishment [will turn upon my head.]
7. *ut-ta-ṣi*	7. Shall I escape .... ? »
8. *ib-ḳú-un-šu-ma [id-di-šu a-na šu-ut-ta-ti]*	8. He stripped him [and threw him into a pit],
9. *a-ša-ar mu-ú-[ut bu-bu-ti ù ṣu-mi]*	9. a place of death [by hunger und thirst].

Possibly lines 10-11 of this text belong here. See p. 32.

p) **The eagle appeals to Shamash.**

Jastrow frag. Rev. 2-5. *Morgan* IV 2, Rev. V (?) 10-14. *)

Pl. III 25-28 = Jastrow frag., Rev. 3-5.

25. ....*ti?* [2]) *erû û-me-šam-ma im-da-na-ḫa--ra* *ilu**Šamša* (*ša*)	25. (*In distress*) the eagle appealed daily to Shamash:-
26. [*i-*]*na šu-ut-ta-ti a-ma-ta-ma: man-nu i-di ki-i šak-na-ku še-rit*(!)*-ka*	26. « Shall I die in the pit? Who knows how thy punishment has been laid upon me?
27. *ja-a-ši erâ bul-liṭ-an-ni-ma*	27. Save the life of me, the eagle.
28. *a-na û-mi da-ru-ú-ti zi-kir-ka lu-uš-te-eš-me* [3])	28. Unto days of eternity thy name will I cause to be heard. »

[1]) For *ma-a* introducing direct discourse, see Tammuz and Ishtar, 145, n. 4; *Epic of Creation,* 204, 109; 206, 120.

[2]) Or *AN?* Var. below, l. 10, *pa-ḫa-zi-iš*. It is possible that the line began *ina* ...... *ti,* or that *ilu**erû* is the reading. Cf. *ilu**Zu-u,* p. 23, 13. Jastrow copied *NITAḪ* for *rit,* l. 26 and the photograph is not clear, but cf. p. 30, 20-21. He divided 26[b] into *man-nu i-di-ki i-šak-na tuš-še arad-ka* and translated « he who stirred up should settle the strife of thy servant »; in any case totally erroneous. Frank wants to read *šak-na ku-bu ardi-ka,* but the photograph has *še* not *bu.*

*) Lines 10-11 may belong to section o) and describe the misery of the eagle in the pit.

[3]) First legible sign on K. 1547, Reverse.

Old version, *Morgan* IV 2, Rev. V (?), 10-14.

10. *pa-ḫa-zi-iš* [1]) *e-ri-[i*	10. ....
11. *ša-pi-il ši-ma*	11. Deep(?) is the ....
12. *û-mi-ša-am-ma [e-ru-u im-da-na-ḫa-ra Ša-am-ša]*	12. Daily [the eagle appealed to Shamash] :-
13. *ša-am-ša ga-ti ṣa-[bat-mi]*	13. « O Shamash take me by my hand.
14. *ja-ti-i e-[ra-am bul-liṭ-an-ni]*	14. Save the life of me, the eagle. »

q) **Shamash refuses help, but suggest a « man » whom he will send to him.**

Jastrow fragment, Rev. 7-11. *Morgan* IV 2, Rev. V (?) 15-17; K. 1547, Rev. 2-6. *)

Plate III 29-33 = Jastrow fragment, Rev. 7-11.

29. *iluŠamaš pâ-šu epuš-ma a-na erî i-zak-kar-šù*	29. Shamash opened his mouth, saying unto the eagle:
30. *lim-ni-ta-ma kab-ta-ti tu-šam-ri-iṣ*	30. « Thou hast caused heavy evils to be committed, bringing sorrow.
31. *an-zil-la šà ilāni a-sak-ku ta-kul*	31. A thing inhibited by the gods, a disgraceful thing, hast thou done [2])
32. *ta-ma-ta-a-ma* [3]) *la-a-sa-an-ni-ḳa-ak-ka* [3])	32. Thou didst swear and verily I will visit it upon thee.

[1]) The line may have no connection with l. 25 above. *erî* seems to be a genitive depending upon *paḫaziš*.

*) The last legible line on K. 1547 Obv. = Pl. II 7 and hence lines 8-28 are completely destoyed between Obv. and Rev. on K. 1547.

[2]) Cf. p. 13, 7.

[3]) Jastrow and Frank translate « thou shalt die », and Jastrow reads *la a-sa-an-ni ḳa-aḳ-ḳa* (sic!)-[*ri*], « to the unseen land ». Frank, *la a-sa-an-ni ḳa-ak-ka,* « I will not remove thy cord ».

33. *a-lik a-me-la šà a-šap-pa-rak-ka ḳat-ka li-iṣ-bat*	33. Go to a man whom I shall send thee; let him take hold of thy hand. »[1])

Old version, *Morgan* IV 2, Rev. V (?) 15-17.

15. *iluŠamšu pi-i-šu i-pu-[uš-ma a-na e-ri-i i-zak-kar-šu]*	15. Shamash opened his mouth, saying to the eagle:
16. *li-im-ni-ti-ma [kab-ta-ti tu-šam-ri-iṣ]*	16. « Thou hast caused heavy evils to he committed, bringing sorrow.
17. *an-zi-lam ša i-[la-ni a-sak-kam ta-kul]*	17. A thing inhibited by the gods, a disgraceful thing hast thou done ».

r) **There was Etana who prayed daily to Shamash for the birth of a son.**

Jastrow fragment, Rev. 12-18. K. 1547, Rev. 7-16.

Pl. III 34-40 = Jastrow fragment, Rev. 12-18.

34. *iluE-ta-na û-me-šam-ma im-ta-aḫ-ḫa-ra iluŠamši(ši)*	34. Etana prayed daily unto Shamash:-
35. *ta-kul iluŠamaš ku-bur*[2]) *šu-'-e-a: irṣi-tum*[3]) *taš-ti-i da-am az-li-ja*	35. « Thou hast eaten the fattail of my sheep: the earth has drunk the blood of my lambs.[4])

[1]) In the original legend, Tablet III, p. 39, probably followed on directly here.

[2]) For *kubur zibbati*. See Holma, *Körperteile*, 142.

[3]) K. 1547 Rev. 9, *ir-ṣi-ti*.

[4]) Primitive conceptions concerning the use of blood are almost entirely absent in Babylonian religion. This is clearly due to Sumerian influence on that branch of the Semitic race. The drinking of blood is forbidden in the

36. *ilāni ú-kab-bit* [1]) *e-ṭim-me* [2]) *ap-laḫ*	36. I have honoured the gods and revered the shades of the departed.
37. *ig-dam-ra maš-šak-ki-ja ša-ilāti*	37. The women diviners have carried out my libations.
38. *az-li-ja ina* [3]) *ṭu-ub-bu-ḫi ilāni ig-dam-ru* [4])	38. My lambs, by their slaughter, have satisfied the

Bilingual Book of Proverbs, see my *Babylonian Wisdom,* 83 § 18 = AJSL 28, 219, *da-ma la tešta.* Here the blood is given over to the earth, and there is certainly a connection here between the primitive Semitic custom of pouring the blood upon the earth, or upon the sacred stones or upon the stones of the altar. In any case it is not the blood upon which Shamash feeds but upon the parts of the animals burned on the altar. This reference to the drinking of blood by the earth, i. e., by the deities of earth, is, to my knowledge, the only trace of the early Semitic rite in cuneiform literature. It does tell us, however, what was done with blood. There is no trace of the Hebrew custom of pouring blood upon the altar, or of giving it to deities by the medium of sacred stones. See R. C. Thompson, *Semitic Magic,* 181. The only trace of the purificatory use of blood is in CT. 17, 5, 50-1, where the blood of a pig is [sprinkled] on the side of a bed, but even there it is a minor part of the ritual, the heart and limbs of the pig being also used. The principal part of this ritual is the use of pure water.

[1]) See p. 23, l. 13.

[2]) Worship of the shades of the dead ancestors formed a part of Sumero-Babylonian religion as important as the evil rôle which the ghosts (*eṭimmê*) of the dead occupied in magic. See *Babyloniaca,* VI 193-215.

[3]) Var. K. 1547, Rev. 12 *i-na.*

[4]) Line 37 refers to Etana's faithful adherence to the practices of divination, whereby he discovers the divine will, more especially by oneiromancy. For the *maššaku* as the libation, or meal offering by which the *šā'ilu* priests divined the future, see *Babylonian Wisdom,* 37 n. 8, and for this priesthood as practisers of oneiromancy and augury, Frank, *Studien zur Babyl. Religion,* 16. The Sumerian *e-še* = *muššakku,* OECT. VI 44, 10; *zi-e-še,* Zimmern, *Beiträge,* p. 115, No. 14, 9, is the ordinary word for *šaskû, saskû,* CT. 12, 28 Rev. 24; RA. 17, 127, K. 2740, 10; RA. 14, 23, 36. *igdamru* in l. 38 must have the same meaning as *igdamra* in l. 37. Frank takes *ša-ilāti* as the subject in l. 38 also, and although he renders *igdamra* as I do, he

gods [1]).	
39. *be-lum* [2]) *ina pi-i-ka li-ṣa-am-ma: id-nam-ma šam-ma šà a-la-di*	39. O lord, by thy command may (the child) come forth [3]) give me the plant of birth [4]).

renders, « they appeased the gods by the slaughter of my lambs »; but why not fem. pl. *igdamra* here also if *ša'ilāti* is the subject? *azli* is the counterpart of *maššakku* and the difficulty is with *AN-MEŠ* which corresponds to *ša-ilāti*. *ša-ilu* is written *šà AN-MEŠ* in ZA. 4, 26, 38, where Var. Gray, *Šamaš*, Pl. I A, 54 has *šá-i-li*, whence *AN-MEŠ* has the phonetic value *i-li*. Hence *ša-ili*, « he of *ilu* »! [A word *'iltu*, garment, does not exist, against Jensen, KB. VI 417]. The name of this priest is *never* written *ša-'-i-lu*, and the word may well be for *ša ili*, « he of the god », i. e. « he of the ghost ». See n. 1, page 35.

[1]) Or has *AN-MEŠ*, here, the meaning « ghosts of the dead »? Since *ilāni kamûti*, which rise from the grave, *ana kasap kispi u naḳ mê*, for the « breaking of bread and pouring out of water », are clearly the *eṭimmu*, or ghosts, and *galugigim-ma* = *ša eṭimmu*, is a title of a priest, V Raw, 51 B 50, Syn. *mušêlû eṭimmu*, l. 51, and *mušêlû eṭimmu* is syn. of *ša-i-lu*, CT, 19, 24 B 24, the *ša-i-lu* is probably = *ša eṭimmu*, and *ilu* « god » = « ghost » in this word. Hence the *ša-ilu* is by origin a necromancer. The *maššakku*, then, would be libations of water and offerings of food to the souls of the dead, by which their ghosts were enticed to arise and deliver oracles. See *Babylonian Wisdom*, p. 10.

[2]) K. 1547, Rev. 13, *lí*, my lord.

[3]) *liṣamma. li-ṣa-a nabnîtu*, KAR. 196, Obv. 54; *arḫiš liṣamma litamar nûr ᵈŠamši*, l. 56; cf. l. 69; Rev. I 1; II 44.

[4]) This is undoubtedly a reference to a plant which aids women in childbirth as line 40 proves. Etana's son *Baliḫ, Waliḫ*, succeeded him to the throne at Kish. In King, *Chonicles*, II 47, 2 = p. 143 II 2, his son's name is *AN-ILLAD*, apparently *ⁱˡᵘIldu*, who is defined as a deity of the mountains, Deimel, *Pantheon*, 1561. Since *illad* probably contains the root *lad* = KUR mountain, *illad* seems to be Sumerian, and the noun *illatu*, strength, help, etc. is written with the sign KASKAL + KUR (*illad*) as a pseudo-ideogramm. It probably had the value *ildu* = ŠI-NAGAR-BU = *illat kalbê*, Ass. 2559 II 6 = CT. 19, 48 B 24. Hence *ᵈIldu* as name of Etana's son, would be simply the name *Ildu* as a deified king, and Accadian, written with the pseudo-ideogramm *ildu*. Etana's son is then *ildu* « he who is born », and refers to the circumstances described in this poem. Etana had been long childless, and his wife's *biltu* or offspring had been

40. *kul-li-man-ni-ma šam-ma šà a-la-di: bil-ti u-suḫ-ma šu-ma šuk-na-an-ni*	40. Show me the plant of birth: deliver my offspring [1]) and make me a name.[2])»

(KAR. 170 (2),3-4)

3. .... *ja pi-ti kat-ma-ti*	3. « .... my, reveal the hidden things.
4. *bil-ti ú-suḫ-ma šu-ma šukna-ni*	4. Deliver my offspring and make me a name ».

stillborn several times. He now appeals to divine intervention for the delivery of a child. The « plant of birth » occurs in Sumerian, *úù-tud* = [*šam alādi*], CT. 14, 31, K. 4581, Rev. 1, with *únu-ù-tud* = [*šam la alādi*], the plant which prevents birth. Also *úpéš* = *šam erî*, plant of conceiving, *únu-péš* = *šam la erî*, plant to prevent conceiving, with *úù-tud* = *šam alādi*, Delitzsch, *London Frag.*, in H. W. 670. Also the « birth stone » is employed for the same purpose. *záù-tud* = *aban alādi*, CT. 14, 14, K. 4396, 12, syn. *ittamir*; *zánu-ù-tud* = *aban la alādi* = *dāiku* (the slayer), stone which prevents childbirth, *ibid.* l. 13. For *ittamir* in ritual for pregnant women, see RA. 18, 164, 8; 165, 23 and note that Sḥamash is the god to whom appeal is made for pregnant women, Meek, BA. X No. 1; KAR, 196, Obv. II 56 + 59. Birth control by plants and stones was practised by the Sumerians and Accadians. Oefele, ZA. 14, 357 says that, in Greece, λίθος ἴασπις (jasper) was carried on the woman's femur to aid birth. The birth plant is described as the *katimti* or « hidden ...... », in the Old Version, Rev. VI (?) 9. For Shamash as god who delivers childbirth, cf. N. Pra., *Ana-Shamash-lîṣî, Lûṣî-ana-nûr-Shamash, Lûṣî-ana-nûr-Marduk.* In the highest heaven of Anu was the *lu* (?)-*lu-da-ta* stone, KAR. 307 Obv. 30. A Semitic word *luludatu* for « birth », on analogy of *lillidu*, fem. *lillidatu*, JRAS. 1917, 723, 7 seems to be not impossible.

[1]) *biltu*, produce, offspring, with Delitzsch, H. W. 232; Jensen, KB. VI, 108, 16. Dhorme's rendering « opprobrium », *Choix*, 172, is false. See p. 21, 44.

[2]) Cf. *šuma ištaknu* they made a name for themselves, KB. VI 158, 42; *šuma ša darû anaku luštaknam*, I will make an everlasting name for myself, Clay, YOS. *Researches* IV 3, p. 92, 187. On l. 4, see p. 41, 12-13.

s) **Shamash directs Etana to the eagle who will show him the plant of birth.**

Jastrow fragment, Rev. 19-21 = Pl. III 41-43; K. 1547, Rev. 17-21. Assur version, KAR. 170 (2),5-12.

Pl. III 41-43.

41. *iluŠamaš pâ-šu i-pu-uš-ma*[1] *a-na iluE-ta-na i-zak-kar-šù*	41. Shamash opened his mouth saying to Etana:
42. *a-lik ur-ḫa e-ti-iḳ šada-a*[2] : *a-mur šu-ut-ta-tum ki-rib-šà bit-ri*[3]	42. « Pursue the route, pass over the mountain: behold the pit, look into the midst thereof.
43. *ina lib-bi-šà na-di erû*[4] : *ú-kal-lam-ka šam-ma* [*ša a-la-di*]	43. Within it the eagle has been cast[5]. He will show thee the plant of birth. »

Assur version. KAR. 170 (2),5-12.

5. [*iluŠamaš pi-i-šu i-pu-*]*uš* ![6]*-ma ana*[7] *E-ta-na i-be-ri* [*a-ma-ta?*]	5. [Shamash opened his mouth?] choosing(?) [his words?] to Etana :-
6. ....*la*(?)*-ja al-mi la ta-ši* (*lim?*)	6. « ....
7. .... *a-lik arḫa*[8] *e-tiḳ šadâ-ma*	7. .... pursue the route, pass over the mountain ......

[1] K. 1547, Rev. 17, *pi-i-šù i-pu-šam-ma.* See p. 32, 29.

[2] See p. 25, 16.

[3] Cf. RA. 15, 180, 18, *bit-ri-i.*

[4] K. 1547 Rev. 20, *e-ru-ú.*

[5] Cf. p. 26, 7; 31, 8; 30, 23.

[6] Ebeling's collation of the text results in no change of his copy. He says that *uš* is impossible.

[7] Or personal determinive and render, « seeing Etana »?

[8] Written with sign for month!

8. .... *la i-na šu-na ki la ka*	8. ....
9. [........ *a-mu*]*r!*[1]) *šu-ta-ta ki-rib-ša* [*bit-ri*]	9. .... behold the pit, look into the midst thereof.
10. .... *ki-it-ru-ub*	10. .... draw nigh ....
11. ...... *i-na libbi-ša erû na-di-ma*	11. .... therein the eagle has been cast.
12. ...... *šu-ú i-na di-na-šu ša-la-di*[2]) *u-ka*[*l-lam-ka*]	12. ...... he in his decision will show thee (the plant) of birth ».

t) **Etana finds the eagle in the pit.**

Jastrow fragment, Rev. 22-24 = Pl. III 44-46. K. 2606, Rev. end.*

44. *a-na zi-kir iluŠamši ḳu-ra -di: iluE-ta-na il-lik ur-*[*ḫa e-tiḳ šadâ*]	44. At the command of Shamash the heroic, Etana pursued the route, he passed over the mountain.
45. *i-mur-ma šu-ut-ta-tum ki-rib-ša ib-ri: ina lib-bi-*[*ša na-di erû*]	45. He beheld the pit, he looked into the midst thereof; in it [the eagle had been cast].
46. *ul-la-nu-um-ma ul-taḳ-ḳa-aš-šu*[3]) [*iluŠamaš*]	46. Henceforth[4]) [Shamash] had utterly destroyed him.

[1]) Ebeling has collated the text and says that the reading is *ki-is*, *di-is* or *ŠAR-is*!

[2]) *Sic* for *šam-ma ša a-la-di*!

[3]) K. 2606, Rev. 1, *uš-ta-ḳa-aš-šu*. Here are two Assyrian texts, one retaining *št* and the other having the common phonetic change *lt*. Ylvisaker's statement, LSS. V 6, 10, in which he wishes to establish the fixed rule that *št* becomes *ss*, is not defensible, at least not for the literary texts.

[4]) On *ullānumma*, see PSBA. 1913, 193-5.

*) The double column tablet, K. 2606 ends with same line as tablet II of the single column edition, Pittsfield + Marsh fragments. K. 2606 cannot possibly be tablet III as indicated by the scribe.

B.

Tablet III of one column edition

a) **The eagle from the pit appeals to Shamash, promising to help the man sent to him** in A, section q[1]). K. 8578, Obv. 1-6.

K. 8578, 1-6, Pl. VIII.

1. *erû pi-i-šu i-pu-šam-ma ana* *ilu**Šamši bêli-šu amatum* [*i-zakka-ár*]	1. The eagle opened his mouth. speaking a word to Shamash his lord[2]) :
2. [*lu-ú?*]-*še*(?)-[*ti-ḳa-an-ni šu-ut-ta-ta*]	2. « May he cause me to pass over the pit(?)
3. [*ad-*]*mi iṣ-ṣu-ri* [*lum-ḫur e-mu-ḳa lu-ši-ì*][3])	3. The young of a bird [may I receive and obtain strength.]
4. [*šà i-*]*ra-šu-ma* [*lu-ud-di-iš-šu*]	4. That which he desires [will I give him.][4])
5. [*mim*]-*mu-ú šu-ú i-gab-bu* [*lu-pu-uš*]	5. Whatsoever he commands [*I will do*].
6. [*mim*]-*mu-ú a-na-ku a-gab-bu* [*lu-pu-uš*]	6. Whatsoever I command [*let him do*].

[1]) Sections r-s-t, Etana's appeal and the direction by Shamash to go to the pit, are really an insertion to explain the reference to *amēlu*, p. 33, 33.

[2]) Restored from catch lines on Tab. II, Pl. III, and K. 2606, Pl. VII. Cf. p. 19, 37; p. 28, 18. JASTROW, BA. III 370, JENSEN, BK. VI 108 had already restored this line almost correctly. DHORME, *Choix* 174, erroneously rejected it.

[3]) See l. 8 below.

[4]) See *Morgan* IV 2, Rev. VI (?) 7.

b) **Etana takes the eagle from the pit and feeds him.**

K. 8578, 7-8; *Morgan* IV 2, IV 2, VI (?) 1-4.
Pl. VIII, K. 8578, 7-8.

7. *ina pi-i ^{ilu}Šamši ḳu-ra-[di ú-še-ti-ḳa-šu šu-ut-ta-as-šu]*	7. By the command of the heroic Shamash [he caused him to pass over his pit][1]).
8. *ad-mi iṣ-ṣu-ri [im-ḫur e-mu-ḳa i-ši]*	8. The young of a bird [he received and obtained strength][2]).

Old version, Col. VI (?), 1-4.

....	....
1. *ga-as-su iṣ-ba-ta-am*[3]) *si-bi su-?*	1. He took hold of his hand. seven? ....
2. *sa-am-na-am wa-ar-ḫa-am ú-ši-te-ga šu-ut-ta-as-su*	2. In the eighth month he caused him to pass over his pit.
3. *e-ru-ú ma-ḫi-ir ú-ku-ul-ta-am ki-ma ni-ši-im na-e-ri*	3. The eagle received food like a murderous lion,
4. *e-mu-ga-am i-šu*	4. and obtained strength.

c) **Eagle asks Etana why he has come to his rescue.**

K. 8578, 9-10 + 79, 7-8, 43, Obv. 1-2.[4]) *Morgan* IV 2, VI(?) 5-7.

Pl. VIII, K. 8578, 9-10.

9. *erû pi-i-šu i-pu-šam-[ma ana ^{ilu}E-]ta-na i-zak-kar-šu*	9. The eagle opened his mouth, saying to Etana:

[1]) See line 2 of Old Version, below.

[2]) See line 3 below.

[3]) Cf. p. 33, 33; 32, 13.

[4]) This text was ingeniously used to complete the ends of lines 9ff. on K. 8578 by E. T. Harper, BA. II 447. All later editions are based upon his brilliant combination of these texts.

10. [*mi-*]*na-a tal-li-ka* [*ḳi-bi-a-am at-ta*]	10. «Say thou unto me why thou hast come.»

Old version, Col. VI (?), 5-7.

5. *e-ru-um pa-a-šu i-pu-ša-am-ma a-na E-ta-na-ma iz-zi-ga-ar-šu*	5. The eagle opened his mouth saying to Etana:
6. *ib-ri lu-ú it-ba-ra-nu a-na-*[*ku*][1]) *ù at-ta*	6. « My friend, verily we are joined in friendship, I and thou.
7. *ḳí-bi-a-am-ma ša te-e-ir-ri-ša-an-ni lu-ud-di-ik-ku*[2])	7. Tell me what thou desirest of me and I will give it thee.»

d) **Etana asks the eagle for the plant of birth.**

K. 8578, 11-19. *Morgan* IV 2, VI (?) 8-9.

Pl. VIII, K. 8578, 11-19.

11. *^{ilu}E-ta-na pi-i-šu i-pu-šam-*[*ma ana*] *erî i-zak-kar-šù*	11. Etana opened his mouth saying to the eagle:
12. *ib-ri id-nam-ma šam-ma šà a-la-di*[3])	12. « My friend, give me the plant of birth;
13. [*kul-*]*li-man-ni-ma šam-ma šà a-la-di*[3])	13. Show me the plant of birth;
14. [*bil-ti u-suḫ-ma*] *šu-ma šuk-na-an-ni*[3])	14. Deliver my offspring and make me a name.
15. [............ *šam-*]*ma šà a-la-di*	15. .... the plant of birth.
16. [*ša iš-tu lib-bi aš-ša-ti-ja*]*a-ṣu-u*	16. [*That which*] *comes forth* [*from the womb of my wife*],

[1]) Omitted by the scribe. Cf. p. 13, 3.

[2]) *Sic*! not dative, *kum*.

[3]) Cf. p. 36, 40.

17. [*šu-ma lu-uš-ku-na-a*]*n-ni*	17. [*Surely shall make make*] me [a name][1]).
18. [*a-lik ur-ḫa e-ti-iḳ*]*šada-a*	18. [I have pursued the route, I have passed over] the mountain,
19. [...................... *šam-ma ša a-*]*la-di*	19. [........ for(?) the plant of] birth.

Old version, VI (?) 8-9.

8. *E-ta-na pa-a-šu i-pu-ša-am-ma a-na e-ri-im-ma iz-za-ga-ar-šu*	8. Etana opened his mouth, saying unto the eagle:
9. *i ni*[2])-? ?*-mi-*? *pi*?*-ti ka-ti-im-ti*	9. .... *reveal the* hidden thing[3])

Here there is a long break in our present material extending over 125 or more lines, of Tablet III of the single column edition. Apparently in this break there was an account of the first ascension of Etana on the back of the eagle to the gate of Sin, Shamash, Adad and Ishtar, where Etana saw Ishtar. *) See K. 14788, p. 53.

[1]) Restorations in lines 16-17 purely conjectural.

[2]) Or *ir*?

[3]) The genitive sing., or « my hidden thing », is difficult. *pi-ti* is uncertain. The translation demands *katimtam*. Cf. p. 36, 3. The line was collated for me by Professor Dougherty. Hardly *bil-ti* after *mi*.

*) It is obvious from the opening lines of Tab. IV that the account of a first ascension must have been given at the end of Tab. III, and in Tab. IV there are two more ascensions. They appear to have started the second ascent, p. 46, 24-37, from the gate of Sin, Shamash, Adad and Ishtar, to arrive at the gate of Anu, after 3 *bîru,* and starting from here they make a third ascension p. 49, 17-26. If the first (lost) ascension from the earth to the planetary sphere (Sun, Moon, Venus, clouds), extended over three *bîru*, the three consecutive ascensions bring them to a height of nine *bîru,* or nearly twenty miles. The second ascent to the gate of Anu, Enlil and Ea (p. 48, 35) brings them to the plane of the fixed stars. But the next ascension brings them to Ishtar and Anu, i. e. to Anu and his consort, and to the

C.

Tablet IV of the single column edition

a) **Comments by the eagle on what he saw at the gate of Sin, Shamash, Adad and Istar.**

K. 8563, Obv. 1-13; Rm. 2454, Obv. 1-7.

K. 8563, Obv. 1-13. Pl. IX.

1. *erû pa-a-šu* [*e-pu-šam-ma a-na E-ta-na i-zak-kar-šu*]	1. The eagle opened his mouth, [saying to Etana:]
2.	2. «[..................................]
3. *ni-rib šà bâb* *iluA-nim* *iluEn-lil* [*iluE-a ni-ba-'a it-ti a-ḫa-miš*] [1])	3. The entrance of the gate of Anu, Enlil and [Ea we will enter and together]
4. *nu-uš-ki-nu*	4. we will kneel down.
5. *ni-rib ša bâb* *iluSin* *iluŠamši* *iluAdad u* [*ilatIš-tar*]	5. The entrance of the gate of Sin, Shamash, Adad and [Ishtar [2]) we *entered*].
6. *ki-ṣir-ta* [3]) *ap-ti*	6. I opened the ....
7. *a-ḫi-ir a-sa-kip*	7. I looked about, sitting down ....

highest heaven, or third plane above the fixed stars. Ishtar in the third ascension, p. 49, 11 is clearly not identical with the [Ishtar] of the planetary sphere, p. 43, 5, i. e., Venus. The third and highest flight is to the region of *Anu* and *Nin-anna,* « queen of heaven », who dwell above the plane of the fixed stars. See LANGDON, *Tammuz and Ishtar,* 87-91, for Ishtar as « queen of heaven », distinct from Ishtar = Venus, the War-goddess.

[1]) Restored from p. 47, 35-6.

[2]) This restoration depends upon the description of the woman and the throne in lines 8-11, where Ishtar seems to be described. See p. 49, 11.

[3]) JENSEN, KB. VI 419, referring to *elînu-ši-na ki-ṣir-tu kaṣ-rat šaplânu-ši-na pitiḳtu šuk-*[*ku-nat*], THOMPSON, *Assyrian Medical Texts,* 10, 1 III 26, concludes that *kiṣirtu* means « eye lid », but this is not consonant with *pitiḳtu* « which is placed under them », i. e. the eyes, contrasted with a

8. *aš-bat ina lib-bi me-lam-me ...*	8. She sat in the midst of splendour ....
9. ......*ru-uṣ-ṣu-na-at*	9. .... adorned [1]) ....
10. *^{iṣu}kussu nadi-ma TI*	10. A throne was placed and ...
11. *ina šap-la kussî la-be*	11. At the foot of the throne lions [*crouched*].
12. *at-be-ma a-na-ku la-be*	12. I went up and the lions ......
13. *ag-gal-tam-ma at-ta-ru-ù*[*r* ... .]	13. I was terrified and trembled .... »

b) **The eagle suggests a second (or higher?) ascent to the gate of Anu. They ascend a double hour's march.**

K. 8563, Obv. 14-17; Rm. 2454, Obv. 8-17.

Rm. 8563, Obv. 14-17. Pl. VIII.

14. *erû ana šà-šu-ma ana* [2]) *^{ilu}E-ta-na* [*iz-zak-kar-šu*]	14. The eagle spoke unto him, unto Etana:-
15. *ib-ri* [3]) *šu-pa-a*	15. « My friend, glorious are the ....
16. *al-ka lu-uš-ši-ka-ma a-na ša-me-e* [*ša ^{ilu}A-nim*] [4])	16. Come, I will bear thee to the heaven [of Anu]
17. *ina eli irti-ja šu-kun* [*irta-ka*] [5])	17. Place [thy breast] against my breast.

kiṣirtu which is « knotted » above them. Cf. *pitiḳtu* placed between them. Cf. *ki-ṣir-ši-na* said of the lips, a condition in which they cannot be opened, « their knot », *Bab. Wisdom,* 56, 23.

[1]) On *raṣānu*, v. Thureau-Dangin, RA. 11, 101. The word is clearly the cognate of Arabic *raṣuna, razuna,* shew oneself dignified, see Langdon, AJSL. 28, 144. Ll. 8-9 = Rm. 2454, Obv. 3.

[2]) Rm. 2454, Obv. 8, *a-na.*

[3]) So Var. 9; K. 8563, *DIRI,* with value *ri?*

[4]) See p. 47, 34.

[5]) Since in lines 21-22 the parts of Etana's body laid against those of the eagle correspond literally to those of the eagle, it is necessary to suppose that *irtu* of the eagle corresponds to *irtu* of Etana, in lines 17 and 20. The

18. *ina eli na-aṣ kap-pi-ja*[1]) *šu-kun* [*kap-pi-ka*]	18. Upon the feathers of my wings place thy hands.
19. *ina eli i-di-ja šu-kun* [*i-di-ka*]	19. Upon my arms[2]) place thy arms ».
20. *ina eli irti-šu iš-ta-kan* [*irta-šu*]	20. Against his breast he placed his breast.
21. *ina eli na-aṣ kap-pi-šu iš-ta-kan kap-*[*pi-šu*]	21. Upon his wing feathers he placed his hands.
22. *ina eli i-di-šu iš-ta-kan i-di-*[*šu*]	22. Upon his arms he placed his arms.
23. *ú-dan-nin-ma ir-ta-bi bi-lat-su: išten(en) bîra u-šá-ḳí-*[*šu*]	23. He was mighty[3]) and great was the load of him. He carried him upward one double hour's march[4]).

seals, Ward, 391, 392, show Etana with his arms about the neck of the eagle, with his breast against the side of the breast of the eagle. On No. 392 his feet seem to meet the claws of the eagle. On the fine seal of the Berlin Museum, Gressmann, *Texte und Bilder,* 1st ed., No. 226, Etana, holding to the neck of the eagle, sits crosswise on the eagle's breast, his legs dangling below the right wing, as on the seal of the Peek *Collection,* Weber, *Altorientalistische Siegelbilder,* 404, after Pinches. It is, therefore, obvious that Etana's breast is placed against the breast of the eagle, sidewise, and that the seal, Ward, 395, showing Etana astride the eagle's back, is not the usual representation in art, nor does it correspond to the text of the legend. Jensen, KB. VI, 102, denies without reason that these seals refer to Etana.

[1]) *kappu* of the eagle, « wing », *kappu* of Etana, « hand ». *nâṣ kappi* only here and below, p. 49, 14. Muss-Arnolt, *Lexicon,* 713, Hebrew *nôṣā,* late Heb, feathers of the body; this is clearly the meaning in Ezekiel 17, 3 (an eagle full of *nôṣā*), 17, 7, (an eagle great in *nôṣā*). *nâṣu* and *nôṣā* are both collectives; see Holma, *Körperteile* 145. Etymologically Jensen's translation « stumps of my wings » is impossible, but it conforms to the scene on the seals.

[2]) The arms of the eagle are the stumps of his wings. Etana places his arms around the eagle's neck above the wing stumps with his hands grasping the wing feathers, his body hanging from the right or left breast of the eagle so that he can look downward. See Ward, *seal* No. 392. Cf. p. 49, 13.

[3]) Pi'el of inner condition; see RA. 12, 79, n. 5.

[4]) ***bîru,* about 6 1/2 miles.**

c) The eagle addresses Etana on the appearance of the world.

Rm. 2454, Obv. 18-21 (= 24-27).

24. *erû a-na ša-šu-ma a-na ^{ilu}E-ta-na iz-zak-kar-*[*šu*]	24. The eagle spoke unto him, unto Etana:-
25. *du-gul ib-ri ma-a-tu ki-i i-ba-aš-*[*ši*]	25. « Behold, my friend, the land, how it is.
26. *ṣu-ub-bi*[1]) *tam-tum i-da-te šá é-*[*kur*][2])	26. Look upon the sea and the sides of the mountain house.
27. *ma-a-tum-me-e*[3]) *li-mid-da*[4]) *šada-a: tam-tum i-tu-ra a-na me-e*	27. Lo, the land becomes a mountain: the sea has turned to waters of ....

d) They ascend two double hour's marches. The eagle addresses Etana on the appearance of the world.

Rm. 2454, Obv. 22-24 (= 28-30).

28. *šana-a bîrā ú-šá-ḳí-*[*šu*]	28. He carried him upward two double hour's marches.
29. *erû a-na šá-šu-ma a-na ^{ilu}E-ta-na iz-zak-*[*kar-šu*]	29. The eagle spoke unto him, unto Etana:—
30. *du-gul ib-ri ma-a-tum ki-i i-ba-aš-ši: ma-a-tum-me-e*[5]) *me-*	30. Behold, my friend, the land, how it is: the land *is like* ... .

[1]) Cf. *ulil-ši ana ṣu-ub-bi-e*, I made it bright to look upon, ZA. V 79, 38.

[2]) Restoration probable. *é-kur*, here in contrast with *tamtu*, means the « earth mountain », the earth as conceived by the Babylonians, and this is its original meaning. *é-kur* occurs on the Assur Etana fragment, KAR. 170(1), 10.

[3]) On *mi*, *me* of direct discourse, see p. 18, 34, and l. 30, below.

[4]) *emēdu*, to attain, stand upon, reach. To attain a condition, «to become». This verb is plastic in usage, but the sense exhibited here can not be illustrated by any other passage.

[5]) On K. 3651, Obv. 1, *ma-a-tū*.

e) **They ascend three double hour's marches. The eagle addresses Etana on the appearance of the world.**

Rm. 2454, Obv. 25-27; K. 3651, Obv. 2-5.

Rm. 2454, Obv. 25-27 (= 31-33).

31. *šal-šá ú-šá-ḳí-šù: erû a-na šá-šu-ma a-na ^{ilu}E-ta-na [iz-zak-kar-šu]*	31. He carried him upward three double hour's marches. The eagle spoke unto him, unto Etana:
32. *du-gul ib-ri ma-a-tu ki-i i-ba-[aš-ši]*	32. Behold, my friend, the land, how it is.
33. *tam-tum i-tu-ra a-na iki šá ^{amel}šākini*[1])	33. The sea is turned to a canal of a gardener.

f) **They come to the gate of Anu, Enlil and Ea.**

(K. 3651, Obv. 6-11).

Rm. 2454, Obv. 28-31 + ? (= 34-37 + ?).

34. *iš-tu e-lu-ú a-na šame-e šá ^{ilu}A-[nim]*[2])	34. After they had ascended to the heaven of Anu[3])
35. *ina bâb ^{ilu}A-nim ^{ilu}En-lil u ^{ilu}É-a i-ba-'-[u]*	35. They entered the gate of Anu, Enlil and Ea[4]).

1) Idgr. *NU-GIŠ-ŠAR* = *šākinu?* So UNGNAD, *Hammurabi's Gesetz,* II 170; VAB. VI 386. Cf. *šakkinu,* Lutz, YOS. II 93, 17; *ša-kin iḳ-li,* RA. 16, 146 n. 1. DELITZSCH, *Sumerisches Glossar,* cites a London fragment, nu-giš-šar = *nukaribu;* cf. ^{amel}*lakurubu,* STRASSMAIER, *Darius,* 276, 4; the London fragment has also *ú-a* = *nu-kar-ri-bu.* Cf. ZIMMERN, ZA. 32, 177, n. 2; GADD in SYDNEY SMITH, *Historical Texts,* 92.

2) For this line, K. 3651, Obv. 6-8, has *three* lines!

3) See p. 44, 16.

4) See p. 43, 3. The ascent of Adapa to the gate of Anu, is mentioned in variant versions of that legend; K. 8753, 17, in LANGDON, *Paradis,* 86; Amarna-Canaanitish version, KNUDTZON, VAB. II 964, 19-20; 966, 37-39. Here stood Tammuz and Ningišzida, and these have been plausibly identified with Castor and Pollux, or the Gemini. The gate of Anu may well be

36. *erû* [1]) *iluE-*[*ta-na it-ti*] *a-ḫa-meš uš-*[*ki-nu*][2])	36. The eagle (and) Etana together kneeled down.
37. [*e-ki* [3]) ...... *e*]*rû iluE-ta-na*	37. .... the eagle (and) Etana ....

Here a long break [4]) describing the events at the gate of Anu, Enlil and Ea. Then a fragment from Rev. of a third single column edition, K. 3651, sets in.

g) **Etana wishes to abandon the flight ?**

K. 3651, Rev. 1-3.

....	....
1. *bil-ta* [5])	1. « The load [*is too great* .....]
2. *e-zi-ib-ma*	2. Abandon [*the search for the plant of birth*]
3. .... *ina ṣi*	3. .... »

h) **The eagle suggests a still higher ascent? *) or having returned to earth he suggests another ascent to the gate of Ishtar and then to Anu ? They ascend, one, two and three double hour's marches.**

K. 3651, Rev. 4-24; Rm. 522, Rev. 1-17; Rm. 2454, Rev. 1-7.

4. *erû ki-a-am* [*a-ma-tum iz-zak-kar-šu*]	4. The eagle in this manner [*addressed him*] :

identical with these stars. See Langdon, *Tammuz and Ishtar*, 37 n. 1. But the Gemini stand in the « Way of Enlil », and are known to have been identified with Lugalgirra and Meslamtaea; Kugler, *Sternkunde* II 209.

[1]) K. 3651, Obv. 10.

[2]) See p. 43, 4.

[3]) So. K. 3651, Obv. 11.

[4]) Nearly one half of tablet IV is lost here.

[5]) Cf. p. 45, 23.

*) See p. 50 n. 8.

5. ...... *nu ja-a-ma*[1]) *lu*(?) ...	5. « ....
6. *lu-bi-la-ku-um-ma*	6. I will will carry thee ....
7. [*ni-i*]*l*[2]) *-lik-ma e-*	7. *We shall go* ....
8. *erû iṣ-ṣu-ra*	8. The eagle a bird [*which* rivals *him has not*],[3])
9. *ul i-ba-aš-ši*	9. [*and another to help thee*] there is not.
10. *al-ka ib-ri* [*lu-uš-ši-ka-ma ana šame-e ša* ^{ilu}*A-nim*]	10. Come, my friend, [I will bear thee *to the heaven of Anu*][4])
11. *it-ti* ^{ilat}*Ištar bêlit*	11. With Ishtar, the queen ......
12. *ina li-it*[5]) ^{ilat}*Ištar bêlit*	12. In the presence of Ishtar, the queen ....
13. *ina eli idi-ja* [*šu-kun idi-ka*]	13. Upon my arms [place thy arms][6]).
14. *ina eli na-aṣ kap-pi-ja* [*šu-kun kap-pi-ka*]	14. Upon the feathers of my wings [place thy hands. »][7])
15. *ina eli idi-šu iš-ta-kan* [*idi-šu*]	15. Upon his arms he placed [his arms.]
16. *ina eli na-aṣ kap-pi-šu* [*iš-ta-kan kap-pi-šu*]	16. Upon his wing feathers [he placed his hands]
17. *iš-ten*[8]) *ana bîri* [*ú-ša-ḳí-šu*]	17. He carried him upward one double hour's march.

[1]) DHORME takes this word as acc. of *jāmu*, sea. But *ja-a-ma* = *ajjamma*, anything, UNGNAD, *Briefe*, 309; ZDMG. 69, 512.

[2]) Uncertain. This DHORME's reading.

[3]) JENSEN takes ll. 8-9 as an address of Etana to the eagle. For restoration, cf. p. 19, 21. [4]) Uncertain. Cf. p. 44, 16.

[5]) *ina li-it* « in the presence of », beside; RA. 23, 104, note 6, with several references by C. J. GADD. JENSEN, KB. VI^2, 5* has corrected his rendering of this passage. For *ana li-it*, see also LUTZ, PBS. I^2, 67, 6; *ul illak aḫatu ana li-it aḫati-ša*, One (eye) moves not in accord with its companion, THOMPSON, AMT. 10 III 19.

[6]) See p. 45, 19. [7]) See p. 45, 18.

[8]) Traces on K. 3651. Var. Rm. 522,6, *iš-ten*. Cf. p. 45, 23 = Rm. 2,454, Obv. 17. K 3651 adds the ideogram for *išten*!

JENSEN, having in mind the arithmetical expression on boundary stones *ana ammat rabîtum*, reads *ana bîri*. Same construction, l. 21.

18. *ib-ri nap-lis*[1]*-ma ma-a-tam ki-[i i]-ba-aš-ši*][2]	18. « My friend, look upon the land, how it is.
19. *šá ma-a-ti i-ḫa-am-bu*[...... *ša*]	19. Of the land [*its* ....] are ....
20. *ù tam-tu rapaš-tum ma-la tar-ba-ṣi*	20. and the wide sea is like a cattle barn ».
21. *ša-na-a ana bîri* [*ú-ša-ḳí-šu*][3]	21. He carried him upward two double hour's marches.
22. *ib-ri nap-li-is-ma ma-a-tu*[4] *ki-i* [*i-ba-aš-ši*]	22. « My friend, look upon the land, how it is.
23. *it-tu-ru*[5] *ma-a-tu a-na mu-sa-ri-e*	23. The land is turned to a garden. ....
24. *ù tam-tu*[6] *rapaš-tu ma-la bu-gi-in-ni*	24. and the wide sea is like a wicker basket ».
25. *šal-šá bîrē* [*ú-ša-ḳí-šu*][7]	25. He carried him upward three double hour's marches.
26. *ib-ri nap-li-is ma-a-tu ki-i*[8]	26. « My friend, look upon the land, how it .... »

i) **Etana refuses to ascend higher and they descend to the earth.**

Rm. 522, Rev. 16-19; 2,454, Rev. 8-21. Lines numbered to continue K. 3651.

27. *ap-pal-sa-am-ma ma-a-tu ki-[i]*	27. « I see the land, how it ......

[1]) Var. Rm. 2,454, Rev. 1, *li-is.*

[2]) Here begins Rm. 2,454, Rev. 1, near middle of the column. Since with K. 3651 and Rm. 522 we are now near the middle of these two fragments, the text of these two fragments published by Harper, BA. II 459 must be *Reverse* in both cases. This is proved by the traces on Obv. of K. 3651 = ll. 30-36 of the Obv. of the restored text.

[3]) Ll. 20-21 = Rm. 2,454, Rev. 3.

[4]) Rm. 2,454, Rev. 4, *tum.*

[5]) *it-tur;* Rm. 522, 12; 2,454, Rev. 5. Cf. p. 47, 33.

[6]) Vars. *tum.*

[7]) Rm. 2,454, Rev. 6 b.

[8]) By comparing the two accounts of the ascensions, (1) p. 46, 24-37 (2) p. 49, 17-26, it would appear that the second account begins the ascent from where the first leaves off, i. e., from the gate of Anu (48, 35), for three *bîru upward.* Cf. 46, 27, after one *bîru* the land looks like a mountain, but

28. *ù tam-tum rapaš-tum ul i-šib-ba-a [i-na-ja?]*[1]	28. and [my eyes] are not satiated with the wide sea.
29. *ib-ri ul e-li a-na šame-e*	29. My friend, I will not ascend to heaven.
30. *šu-kun kib-su lu-tàl*[2]*-[lak? ...]*	30. «Take the way; *verily will I go* ....»
31. *iš-ten bîra is-su-ka-[am-ma]*	31. One double hour's march they fell.
32. *erû im-ḳu-ut-ma im-da-ḫar-šu ina [eli-šu?]*	32. The eagle plunged downward and he kept pace with him [*upon him*].
33. *ša-na-a bîrē is-su-ka-[am-ma]*	33. Two double hour's march they fell.
34. *erû im-ḳu-ut-ma im-da-ḫar-šu ina [eli-šu?]*	34. The eagle plunged downward and he kept pace with him [*upon him*].
35. *šal-šá bîrē is-su-[ka-am-ma]*	35. Three double hour's marches they fell.
36. *erû im-ḳu-ut-ma im-da-ḫar-[šu ina eli-šu?]*	36. The eagle plunged downward and he kept pace [with him *upon him*].
37. ...... *gas*[3]) *a-na ḳak-ka-ri [ša iluA-nim?]*	37. ...... upon the *region* [of Anu?][4])

50, 20, after one *bîru* the sea looks like a barn; 47, 33, after three *bîru* the sea looks like a canal, but 50, 24 like a basket after two *bîru*.

[1]) Or *panū-a,* as KB. VI, 226, 28. *panû* demands Pl. verb. This JENSEN'S restoration. Etana cannot see the sea at all.

[2]) *PI! šakānu kibsu* can hardly mean « halt » as JENSEN suggests. Certainly KB. VI 160, 4, is *ša-kin kib-su,* « trampling », « treading a way ». Cf. *šikin šêpê-ši-na šukbusu kalbi,* whose footsteps tread on dogs, THUREAU-DANGIN, *Sargon,* 375; *šêpê-ki šukni,* « set thy feet », take the route, come, *Maḳlu* V 25.

[3]) The sign before *gas, gaz, kas* is clearly *ur* preceded by a small sign exactly as HARPER's copy. It looks like *igi + ur,* i. e., *ḫul.* Harper's *it-taš-ḳaš* is impossible. Perhaps Sumerian for *limniš iggaṣṣaṣ!*

[4]) If the theory of three upward stages (v. p. 50 n. 8; p. 42 n. *) be true, then the descent through 3 *bîru* brings them to the gate of Anu, Enlil and

38. *erû im-ḳu-ut-ma im-da-[ḫar-šu ina eli šu?]*	38. The eagle plunged downward and he kept pace with him [*upon him?*]
39. ...... *ma erû i-tar-rak: šá E-ta-[na* ....]	39. .... and the eagle *floundered:* the .... of Etana ....
40.	40. ....
41. .... *rid ka-ta*	41. ....

Here the Rev. of Tab. IV made up by the Reverses of K. 3651 and Rm. 2,454 breaks away; but few lines can be missing here. In this break stands the Rev. of K. 8563.

2. .... *nu*	1. ....
3. *[mar-]ḫi-is-su*[1]) *ana ša-šu-ma [a-na* *iluE-ta-na iz-zak-kar-šu]*	2. His wife [spoke] unto him, [unto Etana]:-[2])
4. ....*? tu ja-a-ši bit?*	3. « .... me the house of .....
5. *kima E-ta-ni*[3]) *mu-ti-ja*	4. Like Etana, my husband, [*shall I die?*]
6. *kima ka-a-ši*	5. Like thee [*shall I* ....*?*]
7. *iluE-ta-na šar-ru*	6. Etana, the king, ...
8. *e-ṭim-mu-šu*	7. His ghost ....
9. *ù lip-šu-ur ina bît*	8. And it will deliver in the house of ....

With the end of Tab. IV the legend seems to have ended. Where then can be placed the fragment, K. 14788? which mentions Kish, and from the phrases, *i-na li-ib-bi-šu, az-mu-ur,* is proved to be a poem,

Ea, p. 48, 35. This is the plane of the constellations, which are often called *ḳakḳaru*. See WEIDNER, *Handbuch der Babylonischen Astronomie,* 135. Line 38 clearly suggests a further fall after 3 *bîru*.

1) Cf. p. 12, 2.

2) Cf. p. 46, 24.

3) This is the first examples of a Semiticised inflexion of this name.

and not an historical document. *[ilu]E-ta-na* occurs twice on it. From the point where Etana first appears, p. 33, 34, there is not place for it in Tab. II, and it is unlikely that Tab. III, of which nearly three quarters is lost, referred to Etana and his doings at Kish; for he has already asked the eagle to bring him to the plant of birth. *azmur*, « I sang », indicates some other person than Etana on this fragment. Perhaps it belongs to another poem. With the fragment, VAT 10529 = KAR. 170 (1), I can do nothing. From the publication it seems to be the Rev. of KAR. 170 (2), which belongs near the end of Tab. II. Here a ritual with seven loaves of bread (*sibitti akalē telikḳi*, l. 6) is mentioned, and consequently this fragment may belong in the lost portion of Tab. III, before the ascension to heaven, and describe preparations for the flight to heaven. Cf. l. 4 *[šir]kašadi*; l. 5, *ana pan [ilu]Šamši tukân.*

Nota bene. On p. 52, 39, *itarrak*, from *tarāku*, « sink, fall », see UNGNAD, ZA. 38, 197.

A seal from Kish, excavated at Hursagkalamma by the Oxford-Field Museum Expedition, five metres below plain level. The only seal yet found at Kish, the city of the Etana legend. The scene is like that on GRESSMANN, 226. See p. 45.

List of Abreviations.

AJSL. *American Journal of Semitic Languages.*

AKA. *Annals of the Kings of Assyria,* by E. A. Budge and L. W. King.

AMT. R. C. Thompson, *Assyrian Medical Texts.*

BA. *Beiträge zur Assyriologie.*

BL. S. Langdon, *Babylonian Liturgies.*

Choix. Alfred Boissier, *Choix de Textes relatifs à la divination.*

CT. *Cuneiform Texts, British Museum.*

DA. Alfred Boissier, *Documents Assyriens.*

Epic Creat. S. Langdon, *The Babylonian Epic of Creation.*

Harp. *Lett.* R. F. Harper, *Assyrian and Babylonian Letters.*

HW. F. Delitzsch, *Assyrisches Handwörterbuch.*

JAOS. *Journal of the American Oriental Society.*

JRAS. *Journal of the Royal Asiatic Society.*

KAH. *Keilschrifttexte aus Assur Historischen Inhalts,* (Messerschmidt and Schroeder).

KAJI. *Keilinschrifttexte aus Assur Juristischen Inhalts.*

KAR. *Keilschrifttexte aus Assur Religiösen Inhalts,* by E. Ebeling.

KAT.[3] *Die Keilinschriften und Das Alte Testament,* 3rd ed., by Winckler and Zimmern.

KB. *Keilschriftliche Bibliothek.*

LSS. *Leipziger Semitistische Studien.*

Morgan. A. T. Clay, *Babylonian Records in the Library of* J. Pierpont Morgan.

MVAG. *Mitteilungen der Vorderasiatischen Gesellschaft.*

OECT. *Oxford Editions of Cuneiform Texts.*

PBS. *Publications of the Babylonian Section, University Museum, Philadelphia.*

PSBA. *Proceedings of the Society of Biblical Archaeology.*

RA. *Revue d'Assyriologie.*

Raw. H. C. Rawlinson, *Cuneiform Inscriptions of Western Asia.*

SAI. B. Meissner, *Seltene Assyrische Ideogramme.*

SBH. G. Reisner, *Sumerisch- Babylonische Hymnen.*

SBP. S. LANGON, *Sumerian and Babylonian Psalms.*
Shurpu. H. ZIMMERN, *Die Beschwörungstafeln Šurpu.*
VAB. *Vorderasiatische Bibliothek.*
YOS. *Yale Oriental Series.*
ZA. *Zeitschrift für Assyriologie.*
ZDMG. *Zeitschrift der Deutschen Morgenländischen Gesellschaft.*

PRINCIPAL WORDS AND NAMES.

Pittsfield, Obverse.

Marsh
Obv. 1.

Short break before Pl. IV Obv. 1.

Marsh Reverse.

= Pl. V 14, of K. 2527; l. 17 of 1547 Obv.

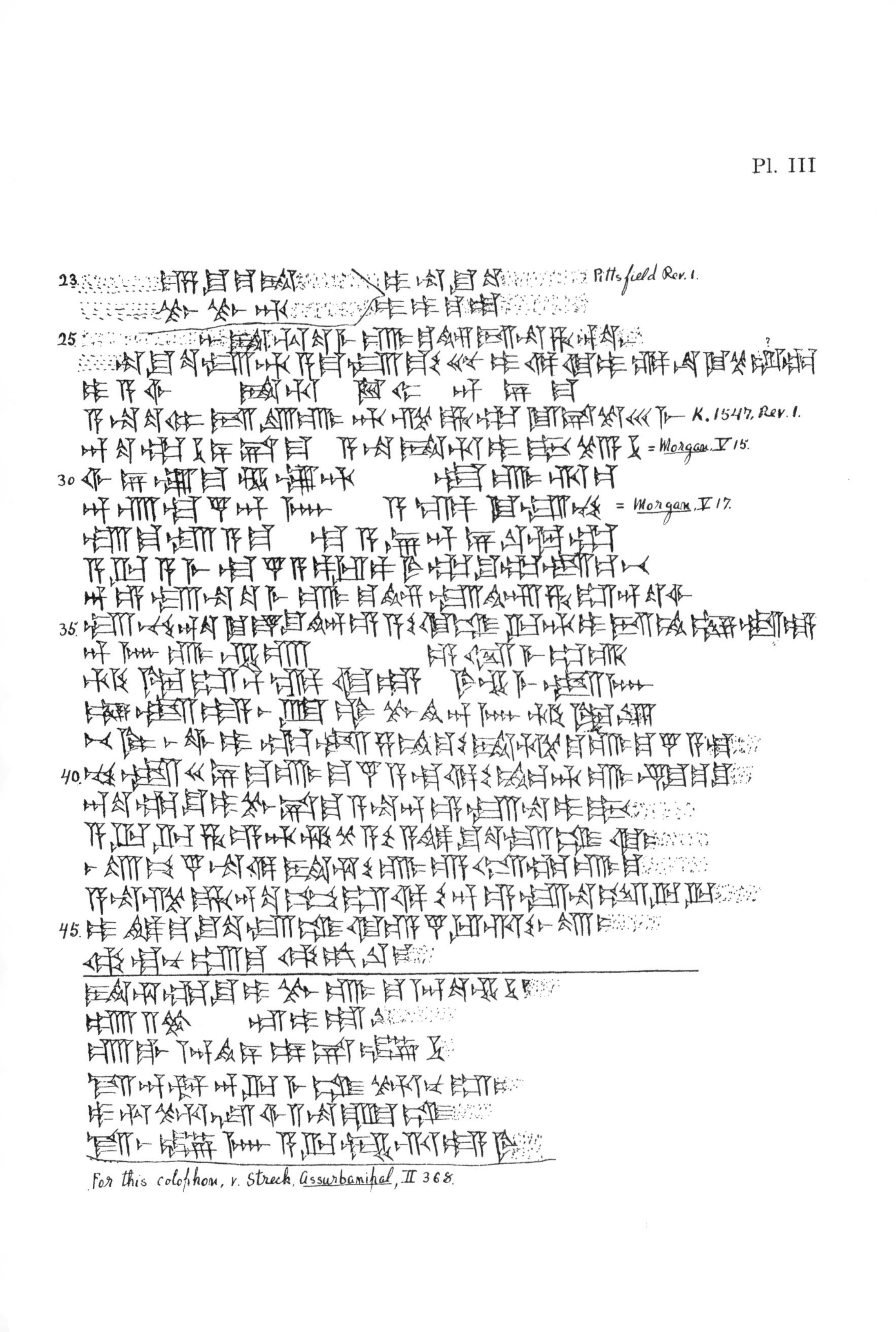

Pittsfield Rev. 1.

K. 1547, Rev. 1.

= Morgan V 15.

= Morgan V 17.

For this colophon, v. Streck, Assurbanipal, II 368.

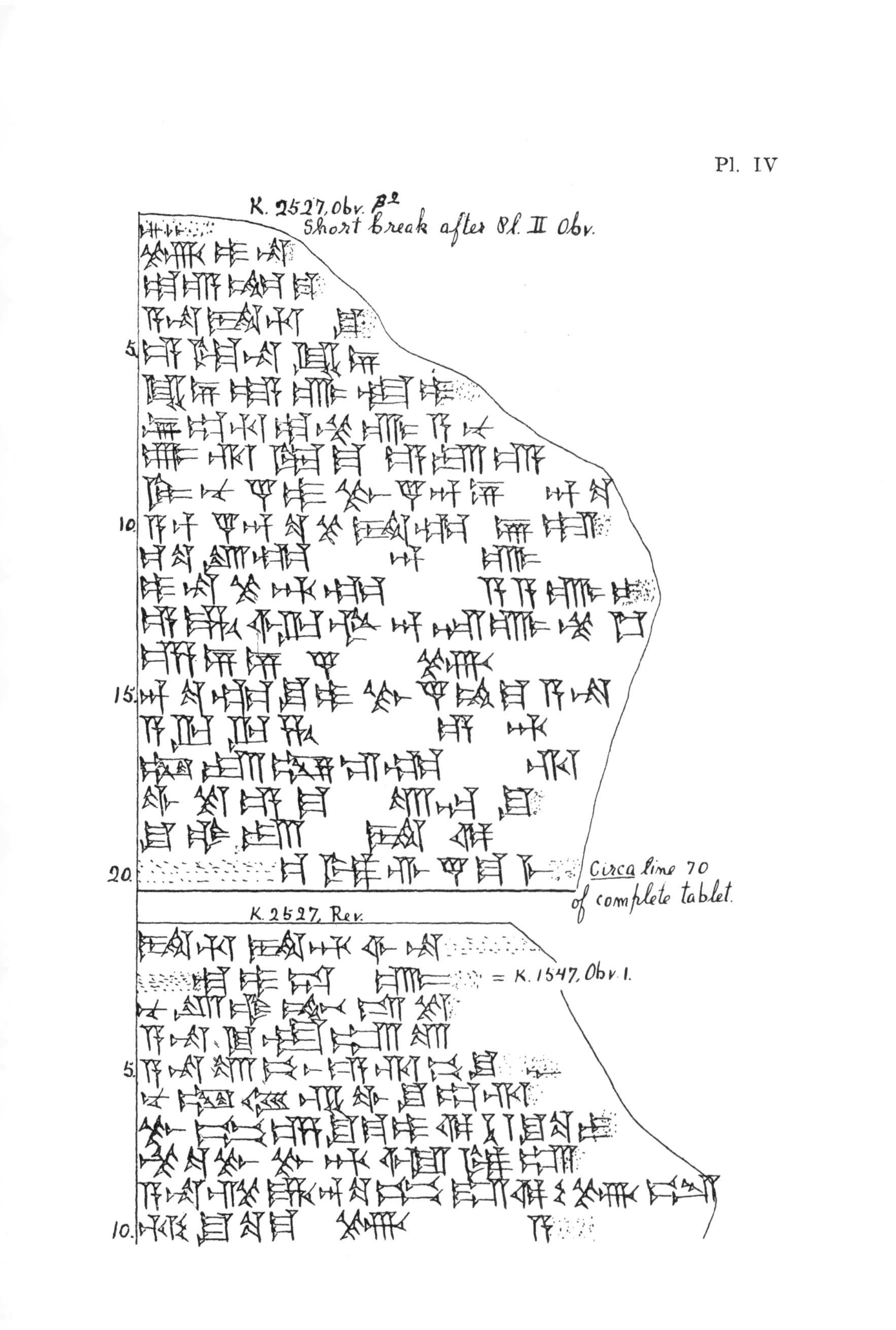

K. 2527, Obv. β2
Short break after Pl. II Obv.

Circa line 70 of complete tablet.

K. 2527, Rev.

= K. 1547, Obv. 1.

K. 2527, Rev. continued.

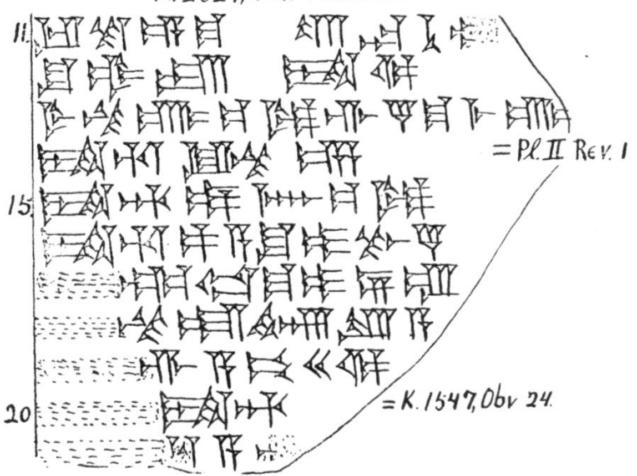

K. 1547, Obv. fragment near end of Obverse.

= Pl. IV Rev. 2.

= Pl. II Rev. 1.

K. 1547, Obv. continued.

= Pl. II Rev. 7.

K. 1547, Rev. near top of the tablet.

= Pl. III Rev. 28.

Obv.

VAT. 10529, after Ebeling, KAR. 170.

K. 2606, Obv. I. (α) Probably Tab. I of double column edition = Tabs. I, II of β edition.

K. 2606, Rev. II.

sic

4

1) end of line 4.

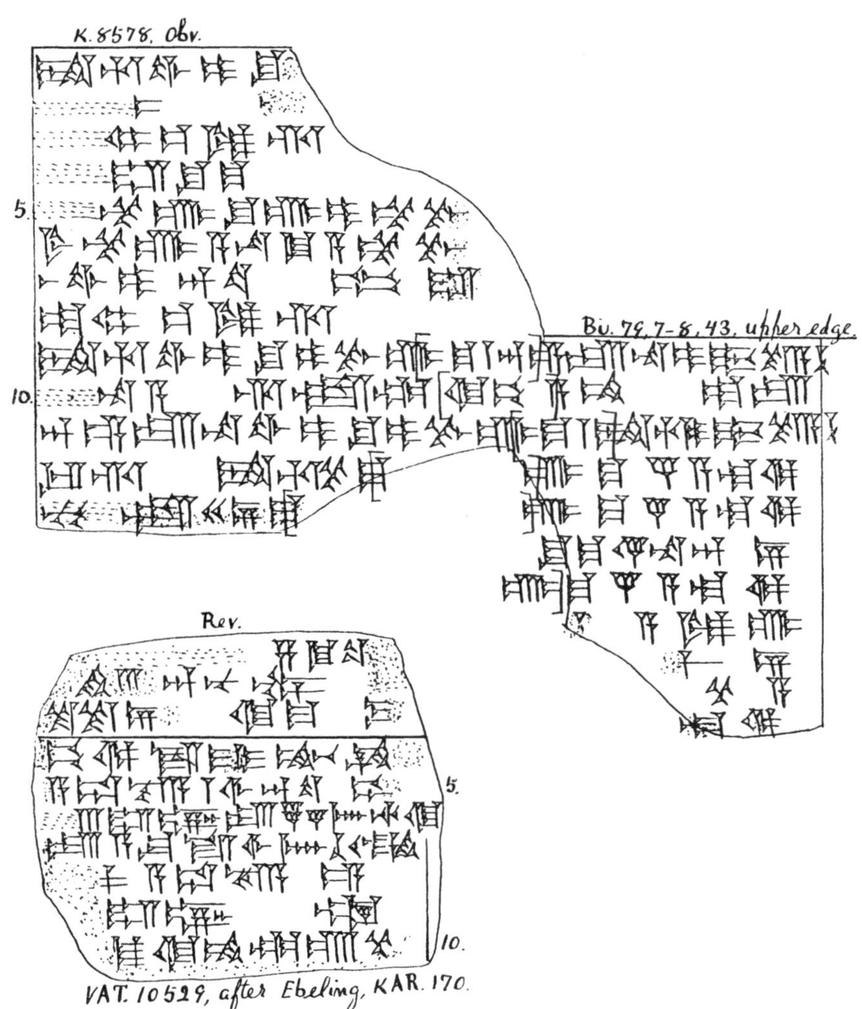
K. 8578. Obv.
5.
10.
Bu. 79. 7-8. 43. upper edge.
Rev.
5.
10.
VAT. 10529, after Ebeling, KAR. 170.

K. 8563, Obv. β'

sic!

*) Only two small signs gone before ru.

K. 3651, Rev. β³.

K. 8563, Rev. β'

Here nine inscribed lines gone.

Line 6 *kima ka-a-ši* has been omitted by error.

Rm. 2454, Obv. 24.b Tab. IV, Obv. 3a

Tab. IV, Obv. 31a.

31b.

32.

Rm. 2454, Obv. 29.

K. 3651, Obv. β³

Rm. 2,454, Obv. β[2]
K. 8563, Obv. 6

Tab. IV, Obv. 8–9.

Broken away about middle of the tablet.

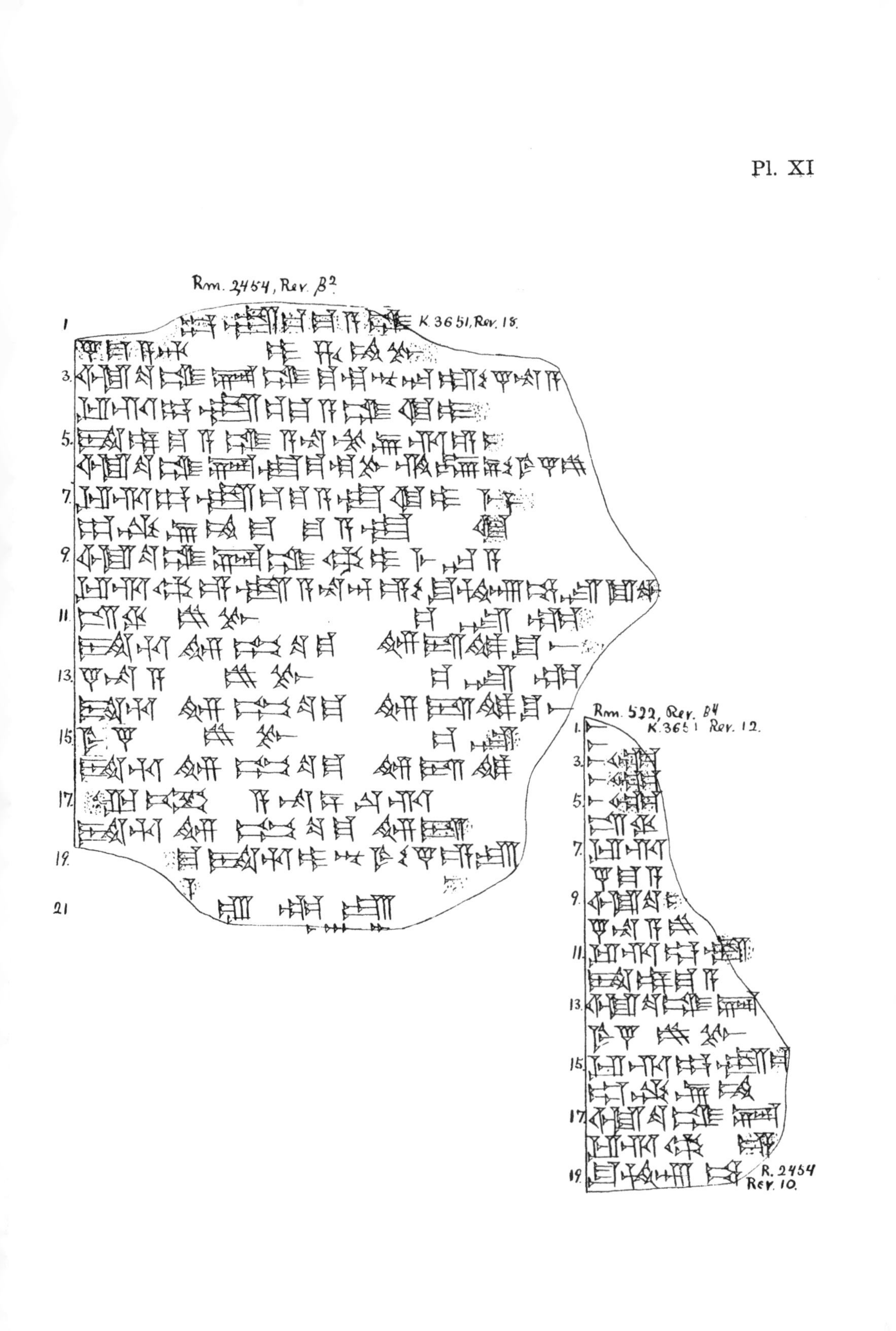

Rm. 2454, Rev. β2

K. 3651, Rev. 18.

1
3.
5.
7.
9.
11.
13.
15.
17.
19.
21

Rm. 522, Rev. B4

K. 3651 Rev. 12.

1.
3.
5.
7.
9.
11.
13.
15.
17.
19.

R. 2454 Rev. 10.

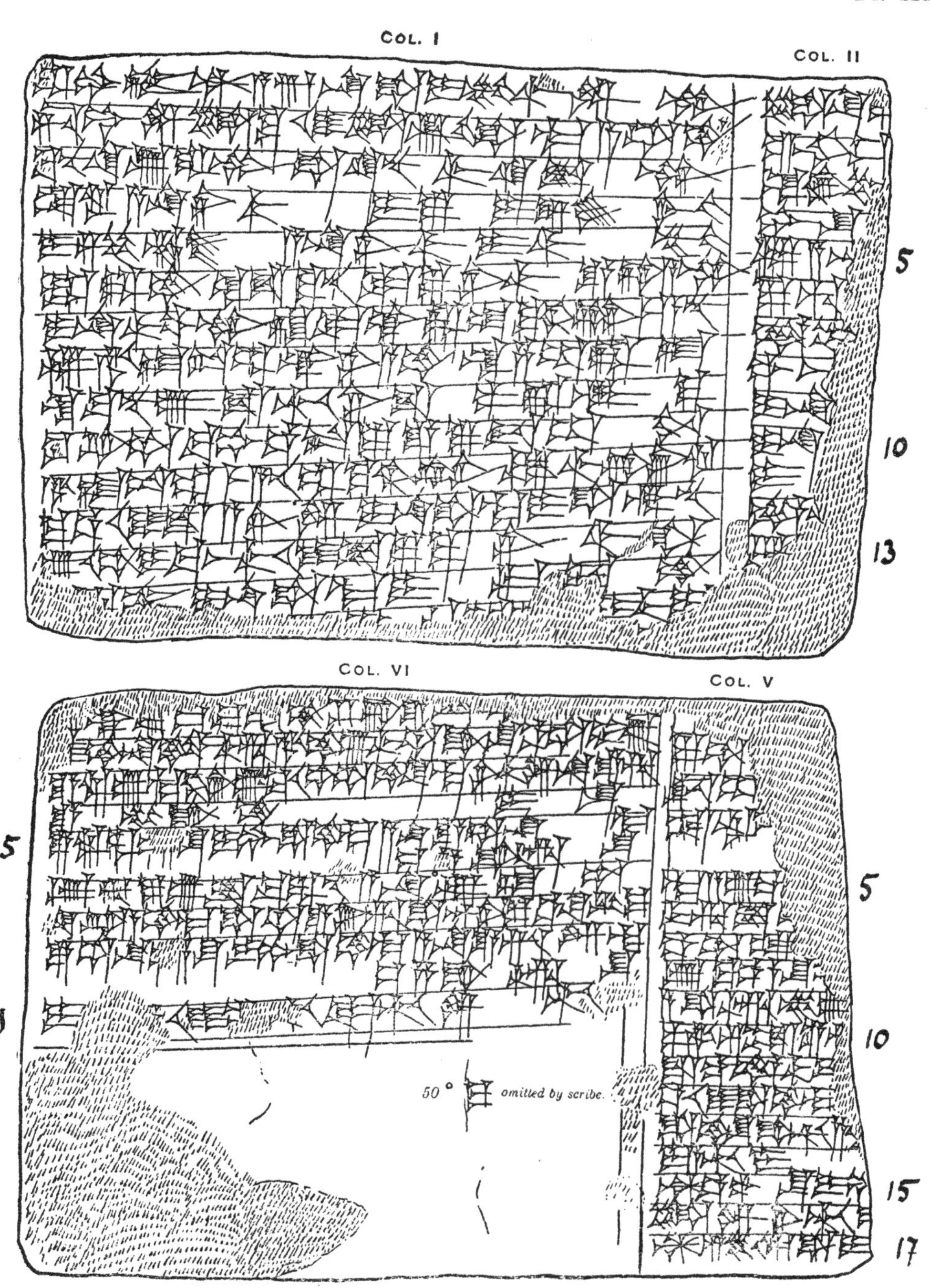

col. VI, 9

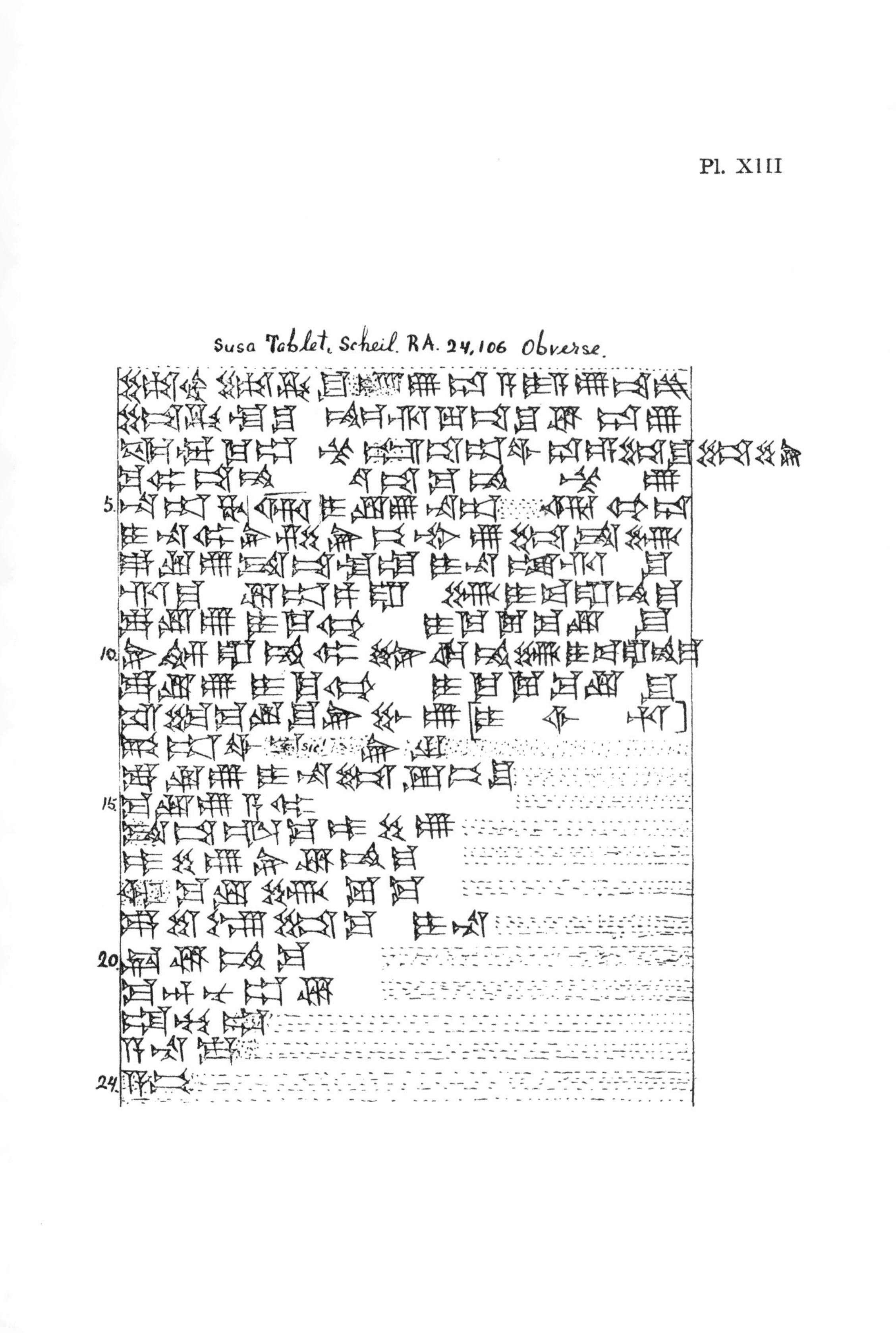

Susa Tablet, Scheil. RA. 24, 106 Obverse.

Susa Tablet, Scheil, RA. 24,106. Reverse

www.ingramcontent.com/pod-product-compliance
Lightning Source LLC
Chambersburg PA
CBHW070745030726
47601CB00001B/150

9781666766950